Points of Entry

POINTS OF ENTRY

ENCOUNTERS AT THE ORIGIN-SITES OF PAKISTAN

NADEEM FAROOQ PARACHA

First published by Tranquebar, an imprint of Westland Publications Private Limited, in 2018
61, 2nd Floor, Silverline Building, Alapakkam Main Road, Maduravoyal, Chennai 600095

Westland, the Westland logo, Tranquebar and the Tranquebar logo are the trademarks of Westland Publications Private Limited, or its affiliates.

ISBN: 9789387578296

10 9 8 7 6 5 4 3 2 1

The views and opinions expressed in this work are the author's own and the facts are as reported by him, and the publisher is in no way liable for the same.

Typeset in Sabon Roman by SÜRYA, New Delhi

Printed at Manipal Technologies Limited, Manipal

To my dearest nephew,
Umer

May you grow up to play your part in building
a more empathetic,
tolerant and peaceful world.

Contents

Timeline

3 June 1947: The British colonial government decides to bifurcate India into two sovereign countries: Pakistan and India.

11 August 1947: Pakistan's first Constituent Assembly is formed. In his first speech as Governor-General, Pakistan's founder, Muhammad Ali Jinnah, describes the new country as a progressive and modern 'Muslim-majority state' where the state will have nothing to do with a citizen's religion.

14 August 1947: Pakistan comes into being as a sovereign dominion of the British Crown. The country has two wings: multi-ethnic West Pakistan and Bengali-majority East Pakistan. Both the wings are separated by a distance of 2,000 kilometres. In between lies India (formed 15 August 1947).

2 February 1948: Urdu (which is spoken by just 10 per cent of the country's population) is declared as Pakistan's national language. This triggers riots in East Pakistan.

11 September 1948: Jinnah passes away.

12 March 1949: The Constituent Assembly passes an Objectives Resolution which resolves to author a

Constitution that will be according to the dictates of Islam. The Hindu, Sikh, Christian and progressive Muslim members of the Assembly describe the resolution as a betrayal of Jinnah's vision. Prime Minister Liaquat Ali Khan assures them that Pakistan will become a democratic and inclusive Islamic Republic and not a theocracy.

4 January 1950: Pakistan becomes one of the first countries to recognise communist China (formed in 1949).

March 1951: The economy enjoys a spike when Pakistan becomes a major exporter of jute (and other agricultural products) to the American troops fighting a war in Korea.

May 1951: A senior officer of the Pakistan Army, some junior military and police officers and intellectuals belonging to the Communist Party of Pakistan (including famous Urdu poet Faiz Ahmad Faiz) are arrested. They are accused of plotting a communist coup against the Liaquat government.

16 October 1951: Liaquat Ali Khan is assassinated by a disgruntled Pushtun nationalist.

12 March 1952: The economy begins to recede as the Korean War winds down. Four princely states agree to become part of Pakistan's Balochistan province.

October 1952: Pakistan cricket team plays its first-ever Test series against India (in India). Pakistan lose 2-1.

February-May 1953: Riots erupt in the Punjab province as far-right religious parties begin a movement against the controversial Ahmadiyya sect. The protesters demand the sect's ouster from the fold of Islam. The movement is crushed by the military. The government rejects the demands of the agitators. Two religious leaders, Abul Aala Maududi and Abdul Sattar Niazi, are sentenced to death for inciting violence against the state. The sentence is later changed to life imprisonment.

23 January 1954: A high-level inquiry report on the anti-Ahmadiyya disturbances is released. It accuses the former Punjab Chief Minister Mumtaz Daultana of fanning the riots (for political purposes). It also holds religious leaders responsible and suggests that they are dogmatic, myopic and a threat to the State.

8-12 March 1954: The country's ruling party, the centrist Muslim League, is routed by an alliance of socialist, centre-left and moderate right parties in the East Pakistan Legislative Assembly elections.

1 January 1955: The country's national airline, Pakistan International Airlines (PIA), is launched.

17 January 1955: Controversial Urdu short-story writer, Sadat Hassan Manto, dies of liver failure brought on by years of alcoholism.

23 March 1956: The Constituent Assembly authors and passes the country's first Constitution. Pakistan becomes a republic. The Constitution declares it to be an 'Islamic Republic'. The country's first general elections are to be held in 1958.

24 July 1957: Leading Bengali, Sindhi, Baloch and Pushtun ethno-nationalists and leftist Punjabis and Urdu speakers form the National Awami Party (NAP). Its main demands are a neutral foreign policy, provincial autonomy and a socialist economy.

17 July 1958: As the Urdu film industry expands, the first version of Pakistan's Oscar awards—the Nigar Awards—are introduced.

7-27 October 1958: Citing political chaos and rising corruption, President Iskandar Mirza dissolves the National Assembly. With the support of military chief Ayub Khan, he imposes Martial Law for the first time in Pakistan. He also suspends the Constitution describing it as 'the peddling of Islam for political gains'. Seventeen days later, Ayub topples Mirza and becomes the Chief Martial Law Administrator and President. He promises to make Pakistan a modern and progressive Muslim-majority country as per Jinnah's vision. All political parties are banned.

8 May 1959: The government bans Pakistan's first 'art film' *Jago, Hua Savera* (Wake Up, It's Dawn). The film is scripted by Faiz Ahmad Faiz and is 'socialist' in content.

1960-62: The Ayub regime introduces various economic, political and social reforms. As parties on the left are suppressed, those on the right (especially the religious outfits) are aggressively sidelined. Pakistan enjoys a period of political stability and unprecedented economic growth. Rapid industrialisation takes root. Pakistan becomes a staunch ally of the United States.

8 June 1962: Ayub becomes chief of his own faction of the Muslim League (Muslim League-Convention). Political parties are restored and the new National Assembly (dominated by Ayub's party) passes a new Constitution. The Constitution changes Pakistan's name from Islamic Republic of Pakistan to Republic of Pakistan.

2 March 1964: Jamat-i-Islami (JI) is the Ayub regime's fieriest critic. It accuses Ayub of enforcing secularism and 'undermining Islam'. Ayub imposes a ban on JI. However, the Supreme Court overturns the ban.

26 November 1964: The country's first-ever TV station is inaugurated.

1 February 1965: Ayub is re-elected as President.

August-September 1965: A land and air war with India ends in a stalemate.

November 1965: The government bans the exhibition of Indian films in Pakistani cinemas.

19 March 1966: Urdu film *Armaan* (Longing) is released. It would go on to become Pakistan's biggest box office hit till 1977's *Aaina* (Mirror). Pakistan's film industry begins its commercial and creative ascent. A song from the film, *Koko Korena* (sung by Ahmad Rushdi), becomes the country's first major Urdu pop hit.

1967: With the rise in tourism, the government strengthens the country's tourism department. The newly-built Islamabad becomes the country's new capital (replacing Karachi).

Early 1968: Pakistan becomes a destination on the 'Hippy Trail'. The trail—on which thousands of American and European hippies will travel between 1967 and 1979—begins in Istanbul (Turkey), enters Teheran (Iran) and from Teheran turns towards Kabul in Afghanistan. From Kabul it enters Peshawar in Pakistan and then from Peshawar it goes down to Lahore from where it enters India and concludes in Kathmandu, Nepal.

October-December 1968: The 1965 war with India had a negative impact on the economy. Left-wing student groups, labour unions and political parties kick-start an anti-government movement which turns violent.

26 March 1969: Cornered by the movement, Ayub resigns. He hands over power to the army chief, General Yahya Khan. Khan imposes the country's second Martial Law but promises to hold Pakistan's first general Election.

May 1970: A magazine published by the American airlines, Pan Am, describes Pakistan as 'a favourite tourist destination in Asia'. The magazine points out that Karachi had 'serene and clean beaches and one of the best nightclubs and bars in the region'. It also writes about the mountains in the north and 'historical Lahore'.

7 December 1970: The country's first general elections are held. The Bengali-nationalist party, Awami League (AL), sweeps the election in East Pakistan. The left-leaning Pakistan People's Party (PPP) sweeps the polls in West Pakistan's largest two provinces, Punjab and Sindh. The leftist NAP and the right-wing Jamiat Ulema Islam do well in Balochistan and North-West Frontier Province (NWFP). The religious parties are routed (along with all Muslim League factions).

July 1971: A vicious civil war erupts between militant Bengali nationalists and the Pakistan army in East Pakistan.

24 October 1971: Pakistan wins hockey's first-ever world cup held in Barcelona, Spain.

December 1971: India joins the civil war in East Pakistan on the Bengali nationalists' side. East Pakistan breaks away to become Bangladesh.

20 December 1971: A group of angry army officers force Yahya to resign. They hand over power to Z. A. Bhutto whose PPP had won the most seats in West Pakistan in 1970. Bhutto promises to 'rebuild Pakistan' through socialism and democracy.

1972: The Bhutto regime begins to introduce populist land and economic reforms.

14 August 1973: The National Assembly (dominated by the PPP) authors and passes a new Constitution. It rechristens Pakistan as an 'Islamic Republic'.

December 1973: With a continual flow of tourists, Karachi is declared as 'the gateway to Asia'. The government forms a special tourism ministry. A leftist Baloch nationalist insurgency breaks out in Balochistan.

May-October 1974: Religious parties begin a violent movement demanding the ouster of the Ahmadiyya community from Islam. Bhutto refuses, but as the movement becomes more violent, he allows an amendment to the Constitution which now declares the Ahmadiyya a non-Muslim minority. A Maoist insurgency in NWFP is crushed.

December 1976: Bhutto announces new elections (nine months before they are originally scheduled to be held). A nine-party electoral alliance of right-wing religious parties and some centrist anti-Bhutto outfits emerges (Pakistan National Alliance, PNA). It promises to introduce Sharia laws and undo Bhutto's socialist and 'secularist' policies, if it came to power. Colour television is introduced in Pakistan.

7 March 1977: PPP sweeps the elections. But PNA cries foul and accuses the government of rigging the polls.

11 March 1977: The Pakistan film industry hits a peak. By now it is churning out an average of over fifty films a year. *Aaina* released on March 11, would go on to run for over 400 weeks!

April-May 1977: PNA begins a protest movement. Bhutto orders a crackdown. The violence intensifies. Bhutto agrees to hold talks with PNA leaders. They demand fresh elections and a rollback of his government's economic policies. They also demand that alcoholic beverages should be banned and nightclubs and bars sealed. Bhutto agrees.

5 July 1977: General Zia-ul-Haq topples the Bhutto regime in a reactionary military coup. Political parties are banned and anti-Zia protesters are publically flogged.

2 April 1978: Pakistan wins its second hockey world cup.

October-November 1978: Pakistan-India cricket ties are revived after seventeen years. Pakistan wins the series 2-0.

4 April 1979: Bhutto is hanged through a controversial murder trial. His daughter, Benazir, and wife, Nusrat, are put behind bars.

15 October 1979: Pakistani physicist, Dr Abdus Salam (an Ahmadiyya), becomes the first Pakistani to win a Nobel Prize. The VCR appears in Pakistani homes. The local film industry begins its decline.

November 1980: Nazia and Zoheb issue Pakistan's first disco album, *Disco Deewane*.

6 February 1981: A multi-party alliance against the Zia regime is formed. It is headed by the PPP and called the Movement for the Restoration of Democracy (MRD).

2 March 1981: Three members of a left-wing urban guerrilla outfit, the Al-Zulfikar, hijack a PIA plane from Karachi. The outfit is headed by Z. A. Bhutto's sons, Murtaza and Shahnawaz, stationed in Kabul. Benazir criticizes her brothers for the hijacking.

3 January 1982: Pakistan wins its third hockey world cup.

8 April 1982: Pakistan's seventeen-year-old squash player, Jahangir Khan, becomes the youngest world No. 1.

August-September 1983: A violent anti-Zia protest movement led by MRD erupts in the Sindh province. Over 600 people are killed before the movement is brutally crushed.

April-December 1984: Zia introduces his regime's harshest policies (all in the name of Islam). Pakistan's NWFP becomes a hub of various Afghan Islamist groups (mujahideen) fighting against the Soviet-backed Afghan regime. Pakistan receives generous US and Saudi aid and arms (largely meant for the mujahideen).

23 March 1985: Zia lifts Martial Law. Muhammad Khan Junejo of a revamped Muslim League is elected as Prime Minister in an election boycotted by the Opposition. Zia remains President.

15 April 1985: Deadly ethnic riots erupt in Karachi between the city's Urdu-speakers (Mohajirs) and Pushtun communities.

18 July 1985: Z. A. Bhutto's youngest son, Shahnawaz, dies under mysterious circumstances in exile in France.

10 April 1986: Benazir Bhutto returns from exile to a thunderous reception in Lahore. She is arrested during a rally in Karachi.

29 March 1987: Zia dismisses the Junejo government.

14 August 1987: Pakistani pop band, Vital Signs, release their first song and video (*Dil Dil Pakistan*).

October-November 1987: Pakistan hosts the cricket world cup with India.

17 August 1988: Zia dies in a plane crash. Sabotage is suspected.

November-December 1988: The first post-Zia elections are held. The PPP (now led by Benazir) wins a majority. The 'Ziaist' alliance, the Islami Jamhoori Itihad (IJI) comes second. Benazir is elected PM. She is the first woman PM of the Muslim world.

1989-90: A wave of pop bands and acts led by Vital Signs emerge. President Ishaq dismisses the Benazir regime. IJI wins the 1990 elections. Nawaz Sharif becomes PM. He resolves to continue 'Zia's mission'. Ethnic riots erupt again in Karachi. Pakistan wins its fourth hockey world cup.

25 March 1992: Pakistan wins its first cricket world cup.

1993-96: The Nawaz regime is dismissed by Ishaq. PPP wins the 1993 elections. Benazir becomes PM again. In 1996, Pakistan hosts its second cricket world cup (along with India and Sri Lanka). The Pakistan pop scene reaches a peak. Over ten million local pop albums are sold and over a hundred pop concerts are held between 1993 and 1996. The Taliban are brought to power in Kabul with Pakistan's help. In 1996, Benazir's estranged brother, Murtaza, is killed in a controversial police raid. President Leghari dismisses the government.

1997-99: Nawaz Sharif's centre-right Pakistan Muslim League-N (PML-N) wins the 1997 elections. Sectarian riots between radical Sunni and Shia groups erupt in Punjab. In 1998, Pakistan tests its first nuclear device. The economy plummets. General Musharraf topples the Nawaz regime in 1999.

2002: Musharraf joins America's 'war on terror'. He outlaws numerous Islamic militant outfits and pulls back Pakistan's support to the Taliban regime in Kabul. He begins to restore ties with India. Becomes chief of the PML-Quaid (PML-Q), which wins the 2002 elections.

2003-2005: The Musharraf regime's liberal economic policies regenerate a depressed economy. He also unfolds various cultural polices that give a boost to the country's music, art and film scenes. He then allows the screening of Indian films in Pakistan to revive the country's cinema-going culture. A string of private news and entertainment TV channels appear. The tourism industry, that had crashed in the late 1980s, begins to slowly restore itself.

8 October 2005: A devastating earthquake hits the northern areas of Pakistan. Some religious leaders blame Musharraf's 'liberal' policies for the catastrophe.

2007: When Musharraf dismisses Pakistan's Chief Justice, a 'lawyers' movement' begins to take shape. Opposition parties join in the commotion, demanding Musharraf's resignation. Islamic militants take over a seminary in Islamabad. Musharraf orders the army to storm the seminary. This results in the creation of the Pakistani Taliban (TTP). It begins to target civilians and security personnel with suicide bomb attacks. The economy begins to collapse. Benazir and Nawaz (now allies) return from exile.

27 December 2007: Benazir is assassinated by a suicide bomber belonging to the TTP. Riots break out all over Pakistan.

February-September 2008: The PPP (now led by Benazir's husband, Asif Zardari) wins the largest number of seats in the 2008 elections. Nawaz's PML-N comes a close second. Musharraf's PML-Q is routed. PPP's Yousaf Gillani becomes PM. Musharraf is forced to resign. Zardari is elected President.

2009-2013: Pakistan is rocked by unceasing suicide bombings and assassinations by the TTP. The economy crashes. Civil-military relations nosedive. The tourism industry too collapses and after 2009, no sports team is willing to visit Pakistan. In 2011, Imran Khan's once tiny centre-right party, the Pakistan Tehreek-e-Insaf (PTI) suddenly emerges with a huge rally in Lahore. PPP man and Punjab governor, Salman Taseer, is killed by his own bodyguard who accuses him of committing blasphemy. In 2012, TTP gunmen shoot and injure fourteen-year-old schoolgirl, Malala Yousafzai.

11 May 2013: PML-N sweeps the elections. Nawaz becomes PM.

16 December 2014: TTP attack and kill over 140 students at a school in Peshawar. The country is shocked.

2015-17: The military (now under Gen. Raheel Sharif) and the Nawaz government launch an unprecedented operation against the TTP militants. By late 2016, the TTP is largely defeated and the number of terrorist attacks drastically decrease. The government also launches a National Action Plan (NAP) to curb extremism. Religious parties complain that it was a way to return Pakistan to secularism. They agitate.

2018: Pakistan goes to polls again.

Introduction

In 1972, I accompanied my mother and sister to Afghanistan. I was just five or six years old at the time. My father—a journalist and a passionate supporter of Zulfiqar Ali Bhutto's Pakistan People's Party (PPP) that had come to power in December 1971—had been posted as a Press Attaché at the Pakistan Embassy in Kabul. We were on our way to join him there. We travelled from Karachi to Peshawar by train and from Peshawar we took a bus from the famous Khyber Pass beyond which lay Afghan territory. I don't remember how many hours it took for the bus to reach Kabul, but I do remember travelling on a whirling road that was hundreds of metres above ground. It was a most fascinating journey.

Just as the bus was about to begin the journey from Khyber Pass, my mother told me that many warriors, kings and traders had entered the area (which became Pakistan) from the Khyber Pass. 'To conquer us?' I had asked. 'Some, but not all,' my mother had replied. 'But many of them stayed here as well,' she had added. I remember asking her, 'Did they become Pakistani?' She smiled and told me, 'No, all this happened before Pakistan was created.'

For years after that trip to Kabul and before I entered my teens in the 1980s, the Khyber Pass stuck in my mind as a point of entry from where everyone wanting to enter Pakistan, came in. As I grew older and began to understand Pakistan beyond the monolithic manner it was taught to us at school, I realised there were so many other points of entry as well in the country (both physical and otherwise) from where numerous peoples and influences from varied regions and cultures had poured in and been absorbed.

Pakistan was created in 1947 as an independent Muslim-majority country. Quite like its larger neighbour India, Pakistan too is a land of some stunning geographical and cultural diversities. The country's state institutions and Constitution encourage the harnessing of cultural, religious and sectarian diversities to create a single sovereign unit based on certain historical commonalities. Or at least now that intent is there. Till the framing of the country's third Constitution in 1973, the state was rather apprehensive to officially recognise (let alone celebrate) this diversity. It felt that highlighting Pakistan's ethnic, religious and sectarian diversity would somehow negate the theory that had rationalised the emergence of a separate Muslim-majority country that broke away from the rest of India in August 1947. This apprehension remained despite the fact that the country's founder, Muhammad Ali Jinnah, had described the new country as a Muslim-majority entity whose polity and state would be inspired and driven by a progressive, multicultural, modernist and democratic interpretation and understanding of Islam.

Jinnah passed away in 1948 and the state's idea of Pakistan shrunk in such a manner that when the country's eastern wing, East Pakistan, plunged into a vicious civil war and separated to become Bangladesh, in 1971, many Pakistanis had already begun to ask, 'What does it mean to be a Pakistani?' A single, immovable idea of nationhood had been constructed by the state and then an attempt was made to impose it upon a diverse population without a democratically achieved consensus.

Thus, the 1973 Constitution—authored by the country's first popularly elected Parliament—provided space to the land's various ethnic groups to democratically contribute to the process of state-building according to their own distinct cultural and ethnic mores. Over the decades, various democratic experiments have been rather successful in at least initiating the importance of yoking together a consensual concept of nationhood built from the unique economic, cultural and political genius derived from the country's various groups. This should have always been the case.

The last manifesto of Pakistan's founding party, the All India Muslim League (AIML), had claimed that a Muslim-majority state (or a state constructed by a minority community in India) was inherently more equipped to appreciate religious plurality, harmony and diversity than a state dominated by an existing large (read: Hindu) majority. The manifesto laid out AIML's idea of the state as something that had a soul. According to the manifesto, the state in the proposed Muslim-majority country would 'be the alter-ego of the national being, and in good time the two would merge to form an ordered and conflict-free society.'

So in all likelihood, Jinnah was already anticipating a diverse country where interaction and engagement between a Muslim majority and other faiths in various economic, political and cultural spheres would be able to construct a dynamic society and state. But, of course, once the minority became the majority in the new country, sectarian, sub-sectarian and ethnic differences came to the fore. And the intensity of these divisions was such that the nascent and inexperienced state of Pakistan fumbled badly in trying to address the issue. It attempted to hastily create a national identity based entirely on a synthetic and monolithic paradigm of nationhood which ended up creating further fissures based on ethnicity and Muslim sects and sub-sects. Unable to appreciate its many diversities, the new majority turned on itself.

The idea of imposing a monolithic notion of nationhood and the state was a cosmetic solution and the results were drastic. Indeed, the country had to be kept intact as a single nation, but the state's idea of this singularity only managed to offend and alienate various distinct ethnic groups, many of who claimed that their histories not only pre-dated Pakistan, but Islam as well! This resulted in episodes such as the 1971 break-up of the country when the Bengali-majority East Pakistan rose up in revolt, and the eventual emergence of religious militancy, which, from the 1980s onwards, hijacked the faith-based dimensions of Pakistan's nationalism and moulded them into meaning a land which was to be forcibly dominated by a very narrow idea of Pakistan's majority faith.

But despite the fact that the country lost its eastern wing in 1971 and then became extremely introverted and even myopic about how it saw itself as a Muslim-majority state, things in this respect eventually began to straighten themselves out. More and more Pakistanis of different ethnicities have become conscious of their communities' histories and many diverse political, religious and social elements have continued to inform and find their voice in what one can now define as 'the culture of Pakistan'. And this did not break the country up. Quite the contrary.

From the mid-2000s the state and government began to gradually return to the narrative of the 'modernist Islam' of the founders that had begun to erode in the 1970s and had been replaced by an entirely reactive one from the 1980s onward. But the new narrative is more pragmatic than ideological. And it has to be, to avoid the more monolithic and cosmetic aspects of the previous strand (of Muslim modernism). It is still very much a work-in-progress. It maintains that to make Pakistan an important economic player in the world, certain radical steps are necessary. These steps include the proliferation of free market enterprise and foreign investment, which, in turn, requires Pakistan to change its internal and external policies and crack down on anything threatening the erosion of local and international economic confidence.

Optimists have already predicted that Pakistan is well on its way to pulling itself out of the quicksand which it created and then fell into; whereas the sceptics advise caution. They say it is just too early to predict anything conclusive because the mountain through which the country is now trying to drill a tunnel, has been piling upwards for over thirty years now. Because despite the 1973 Constitution, the monolithic idea of Muslim modernism has been replaced by an equally monolithic idea of a more belligerent Muslim state.

After years of withstanding religious extremism and militancy (which began to emerge from the 1980s), the new narrative includes a new-found angle on how Pakistan's diversity is to be viewed. Instead of clubbing the country's various ethnic, sectarian and religious groups into a cosmetic nationalistic whole designed by the state, the state is now interacting with Pakistan's latest experiments with civilian democracy and constitutionalism to construct a nation where every group is encouraged to participate in the nation-building process.

This will make the state and government of the country to draw brain and manpower from across Pakistan, giving a majority of Pakistanis a sense of participation and belonging in the state and nation-building process. The hope is that a future Pakistan is not going to be a discordant, alienated and demonised entity rampant with ethnic and religious violence. It will become the Pakistan Jinnah had in mind: a diverse and progressive society driven by a robust economy and a cohesive nationalist impulse built from the unique genius of every ethnic culture and faith that resides here.

My attempt in this book is to fling open the points of entry from where all those people and influences have come in for thousands of years, to help answer that puzzling question which still haunts the country: what exactly does it mean to be a Pakistani?

1

A Past in Ruins

Mohenjo-daro was one of the oldest settlements in the Indus Valley Civilisation.[1] Believed to have been built 5,000 years ago in an area which is today in the Sindh province of Pakistan, most historians suggest that it was abandoned some 3,000 years ago.[2] It remained buried beneath thousands of years of dust, sand and stone until it was rediscovered in 1920 by an Indian archaeologist, R. D. Banerji. Subsequent studies of the site reveal that Mohenjo-daro was a sophisticated settlement of traders, fishermen and farmers. It had a written language (which is yet to be deciphered) and complex religious cults. It was given its name by Banerji. In Sindhi, Mohenjo-daro means, 'the mound of dead men'. The site is located west of the Indus river in Sindh's present-day Larkana district. The Indus Valley Civilisation spanned much of what today is Pakistan, and Mohenjo-daro was one of its largest cities.

In the 1960s, archaeologists who took part in some of the last major excavation works on the site claimed that Mohenjo-daro as a city declined due to the invasions of warrior-nomads of Central Asia (the 'Aryans') who subdued the people of the Civilisation. However, many later-day archaeologists and historians (especially from India) have refuted the Aryan invasion theory. They now believe that the cities of the Indus Valley Civilisation such as Mohenjo-daro began to decline and had to be abandoned due to the river Indus changing its course. They also add that the impact of climate change in the area curtailed rainfall during the monsoon seasons.

I first visited the ruins of Mohenjo-daro in 1974. I was just seven years old and a Grade III student at a school in Karachi. My visit was part of a 'class away day', during which students from Grades III and IV were flown on a Pakistan International Airlines (PIA) flight to Mohenjo-daro in the morning, and then flown back to Karachi in the evening. Then, the PIA used to operate regular flights to Mohenjo-daro (mainly from Karachi) and to enable this, a special (albeit tiny) airport had been constructed near the site. The site was hugely popular with historians, archaeologists and foreign tourists who in those days used to visit Pakistan in fairly large numbers.

I don't remember much about the visit, but I do recall strolling with classmates and teachers on a sprawling site, surrounded by men and women most of whom were quite clearly not Pakistani. I had believed that the tale of this ancient land which we were being taught in class was just another fairytale; but there I was, standing in the middle of the story, clomping my feet on its rough ground, seeing in front of my eyes its buildings and monuments and now I believed the story. I remember concluding that which one can physically feel is the truth; and that which one can't, is a fairytale. Or something of the sort.

The second time I visited Mohenjo-daro was twelve years later, in 1986. By then, I was a second-year student at a state-run college in Karachi. Between 1983 and 1986, I often travelled deep inside the Sindh province, mainly for political reasons. I was a member of a progressive student outfit, and, since in the 1980s the interior of Sindh had become a hotbed of agitation against the Zia-ul-Haq dictatorship (1977-88), members of the student outfit I was a part of frequently travelled to various cities and towns in central and northern Sindh.

In November 1986, I accompanied four other members of the student outfit on a trip to the ancient city of Sehwan Sharif in Sindh's Jamshoro district. Our plan was to join anti-Zia protests being planned by the country's main opposition party, the Pakistan People's Party (PPP) and some small far-left groups and Sindhi nationalist outfits. We travelled by bus to Hyderabad and from there we were to take another bus which would have taken us directly to Sehwan Sharif. Sehwan is best known for its beautiful shrine of the Sufi saint Lal Shahbaz Qalandar. The protests were being planned around the shrine during the colourful and boisterous annual festivities which take place there to mark the saint's mystical enjoinment with the Almighty.

In Hyderabad, some of our comrades warned us that there were rumours that the Zia regime had sent 'hundreds of plain-clothed policemen' to Sehwan who were to begin arresting possible agitators a day or two before the protests. We were advised to stay put until the rumours were confirmed or proven wrong. But, instead of staying in Hyderabad, we decided to travel to Larkana and stay with a friend there. We reached Larkana by bus but couldn't locate my friend. One of his brothers told us that he might have been arrested in a nearby village where he had gone a few days before our arrival.

We ended up staying the night at a cheap, rundown hotel, four of us sharing a room which had just one rickety charpoy, but lots of bedbugs! So we decided to sleep on the cold floor. What helped us sleep better (in fact, sleep at all), were neat swigs from a bottle of the very strong and entirely unsmooth *Lion's Whisky* which we had bought for Rs. 60 from a 'licensed wine shop'[3] situated just behind our Hotel Chaand. The next morning, one of the guys, Rehan AKA *Roosi Sundi* or Russian Insect—because he always claimed to be a better Marxist and 'more *surkh* (red)' than any one of us—rented a motorbike (Honda 70) from a rental-cum-tyre-shop to ride to the village from where our Larkana buddy was supposedly arrested. I accompanied him. We failed to locate the village and were making our way back to Larkana when I saw a board that read 'Mohenjo-daro 20 KM.'

Soon, instead of Larkana, we were riding towards Mohenjo-daro. We reached the site late afternoon. It was breathtaking. Vast and very still. As we made our way towards the ruins, I somehow remembered the spot where I had stood and clomped my feet on the ground twelve years ago. There was hardly anybody there. There were just two gentlemen in the distance standing on a heap of ancient bricks. They were intensely studying what looked like a large map. I think one of them was Japanese. Or he may have been Chinese, I am not sure. Nearer to where we were was a man sitting on a crumbling wall. He was smoking a cigarette and looking straight ahead. His was a rather vacant gaze.

Roosi began walking towards the two map men who were about hundred metres ahead of us, as I made my way to the nearby spot where I had stood as a seven-year-old schoolboy. I stood on that spot and began to gently clomp on it with my feet. This made me smile and chuckle. This was when I heard a voice (in Urdu) from behind where I was standing say, '*Sain,*[4] are you trying to look for oil?' I turned and saw the gazing man now gazing at me. I smiled at him and took out my pack of Gold Flake cigarettes and lit one. I then began to walk towards the crumbling old wall he was sitting on. '*Assalam alaikum,*' I greeted him, shaking his hand. He must have been in his sixties, but his moustache was jet-black, most probably dyed. He was wearing a grey turban and a traditional blue Sindhi *kameez-shalwar* (long and loose shirt and loose, baggy trousers).

He responded to my greeting with a slight nod of his head even as he closely studied me. My longish, unruly hair blowing left to right, my four-day-old stubble, my rimmed glasses, my faded Lou Reed T-shirt over which I wore an equally faded denim jacket; my dusty blue jeans and my beige 'Peshawari chappals'.[5]

'Are you from Karachi?' he asked in his heavily accented Urdu. 'Yes,' I responded. 'Is it that obvious?' I chuckled. He remained deadpan and then began to gaze in the distance once again as he lit himself another cigarette—King Stroke, or 'Bagla Brand' as it used to be known in those parts then—a filterless blast of unadulterated tobacco smoke.

'Are you from around here?' I asked.

He slowly turned his head towards me: 'I used to be a guide here …' he said. 'Nowadays there are more guides here than visitors.'

I nodded my head: 'Yes, looks that way. I first came here as a child in 1974. Were you a guide in those days?'

He softly shrugged his shoulders: 'My memory is not

very good these days. My father was a guide here as well. Many people used to visit this place then.'

'Are you still a guide here?' I asked.

His face lit up with a half-smile. 'I can be if you want me to,' he said.

'I don't have much money,' I said in a rather apologetic tone. This made him laugh: 'Hahahaha ... Sain, who asked for money? This is our motherland.'

I nodded in agreement.

He then added: '*Kya samjhe*, Sain?' What did you understand?

'Pakistan?' I replied.

He began to laugh again: 'Hahahaha ... no, Sain, birthplace of Pakistan.'

'India?' I asked, now a bit more assertively.

He politely shook his head: 'Sain, birthplace of India too. All this ...,' he gestured with a jerk of his head and eyes to me to look at the ruins around us. 'Land of Sindhu.'[6]

'River Indus ...' I replied. 'Yes,' he agreed finally. 'Sindhu gave birth to this place—Mohenjo-daro—which gave birth to India and then Pakistan. Kya samjhe, Sain?'

'What about the Arabs?' I just had to ask this.

'Qasim?'[7] He enquired.

'Yes.'

'He was our guest,' he said, proudly.

'But he invaded Sindh (in the eighth century CE) and defeated Sindh's Hindu ruler, Raja Daher. What do you think of that?' I asked.

He replied with a rather remarkable tale. He said back in 1979, when one of his younger brothers travelled to Oman as an electrician, he was once badly insulted by his

Arab employer. He said his brother scoffed at the Arab by telling him that he (the brother) came from the land of Sindhu which had taught the Arabs many things that they did not know.

'So what did the Arab say?' I asked.

'He actually began to respect my brother! He started to call him Raja Daher.' He laughed.

'Wasn't your brother insulted?' I probed.

The man stared at me with a completely unconcealed what-the-hell expression, 'Sain, why would he be insulted?'

'Well, your brother is Muslim and ...'

Another burst of laughter cut me off. 'Sain, he (Daher) was here before them (the Arabs). He was here before you, who came from so many places in India.' He assumed I was from an Urdu-speaking family which had migrated to Pakistan (specifically to Karachi) from various Indian cities and towns after the creation of Pakistan in 1947.

'Sain,' said I defensively, 'My father is from north Punjab. So I am basically Punjabi. But, yes, my mother migrated from Delhi in India and is Urdu-speaking.'

He jiggled his head a bit: 'Daher's ancestors were from here (Mohenjo-daro). And so were the ancestors of you and me. We all are older than the Arabs. Kya samjhe, Sain?'

I nodded and offered him a cigarette from my pack. He took one and I lit it for him. 'Where have all the tourists gone?' I asked.

He took an intense drag from the cigarette and then exhaled just as intensely. 'Good,' he said, praising the cigarette.

'Gold Flake,' I said.

He nodded and then began to gaze at the sun which was about to set behind the ruins.

'You know what my brother began to call his boss?' he asked. 'Camel driver!'

I laughed. 'Really? And the Arab did not mind?'

'I don't know. I haven't seen my brother for the past three years,' he said, matter-of-factly.

'Why?' I enquired.

'He called his wife and children to Oman and then never came back. He thought this was not a suitable place anymore for his children.'

'How come?'

He shrugged his shoulders. 'Allah knows. My brother began to look at us as if we were from some other land. He also stopped coming here to Mohenjo-daro, even though he once used to love this place. He went away and so did the visitors. Maybe they, too, began to see this place as some other land.'

This made me chuckle. But he remained serious. 'Your friend is a Sindhi?' he asked, watching Roosi walking towards us.

'Yes,' I said. 'He is from Khairpur but studies with me at a college in Karachi'

Addressing the approaching Roosi, he loudly asked him (in Sindhi), 'Sain, what did you learn?'

'I learnt that there is not a single cigarette shop here, Sain!' replied Roosi, equally loudly.

I laughed. So did Roosi. But the man remained serious. 'It's not good to smoke in the presence of one's ancestors,' he said to Roosi, who was now with us.

'But you were smoking,' I said.

'I have lost the respect of our ancestors.' Then pointing towards Roosi, he said, 'But he is a young Sindhi. He should not lose what we have lost.'

In a blink of an eye, Roosi swooped down and touched the man's feet and then his own heart. '*Bhali,* Sain (Sure, Sir),' he said in Sindhi and then softly reminded me that it was getting late. We bid farewell to the man and headed back to Larkana.

From that day onwards, till I last met him sometime in the early 1990s, I never saw Roosi smoke another cigarette again. He quit. Just like that.

Kya samjhe, Sain!

2

White Heat

After overcoming the vast Persian Empire, the armies of the great Greek-Macedonian emperor, Alexander, entered India in 326 BCE. The Greeks believed that the limits of the world ended in India[1] beyond which lay an enormous ocean; and that if they were able to conquer this immense territory, they could then very well claim to have conquered the world. After entering the region through the northern areas of what today is Pakistan, the victorious and ambitious emperor crossed the Indus river and fought a costly battle with the armies of Porus, the ruler of ancient Punjab. The battle took place on the banks of what is today river Jhelum in Pakistan's Punjab province.

The battle, fought at the peak of the monsoon season, was fierce. Even though Alexander won the battle and appropriated Punjab into his expansive Greek empire, he had lost hundreds of men. The rest were left exhausted. Impressed with the way Porus had put up a fight, Alexander offered Porus the position of a 'satrap' (a Greek governor)[2] and made plans to move further ahead. But after the exhausting battle, sections of Alexander's army mutinied and refused to go any further. The young warrior-king implored them to carry on for they were on the verge of 'conquering the whole world'. But close advisors opined that the now fatigued and homesick army should return to Greece and leave behind Greek overseers in the captured territories. Alexander reluctantly agreed.

He decided to sail down river Chenab and then the Indus and exit India by sea. His passage was blocked by the Malhi tribe in the present-day Pakistan city of Multan. Alexander led his forces to attack the main Malhi area which was fortified by a citadel. On the walls of the citadel, Alexander was injured by a Malhian arrow. Believing that he was dead, his forces ransacked the citadel and slaughtered the men, women and children there. Due to the efforts of his surgeon, Alexander, however, managed to survive the injury. But the fight had gone out of him. His forces finally exited India through the Sindh province and the Makran area in present-day Pakistan. When he died in 323 BCE in Babylon, he was just thirty-two.

The citadel on the walls of which Alexander had fought his last major battle and was seriously injured has long vanished. Historians and archaeologists are not quite sure when the citadel was torn down and by whom. But many believe that in its place today stands the tomb of the thirteenth century Sufi saint, Shah Rukn-e-Alam.[3] The tomb was completed in 1325 CE during the rule of Ghiyas-ud-din Tughlaq, the founder of the Turkic Tughlaq dynasty in India. I have travelled and stayed in Multan on at least two occasions, but somehow I never managed to visit the locality where the tomb is situated.

Nevertheless, a very good friend of mine, the late Musadiq Sanwal, was from Multan. An excellent folk singer, poet, author and journalist, Musadiq passed away from cancer in 2014. Some three years before his untimely passing, Musadiq had told me a very interesting story which began at Rukn-e-Alam's tomb, and, apparently, ended in Greece via the picturesque Swat Valley in the north of Pakistan.

In the early 1970s, when Musadiq was at school in Multan, some of his classmates and he knew a man named Noor Qadir. Noor at the time was in his early twenties and was often found loitering around Rukn-e-Alam's tomb. He had studied at a local religious seminary as a child and then went to a government school before quitting in Grade VI, much to his father's displeasure. The father was a homeopath who owned a small clinic in the centre of the city. Noor had a fair complexion and green eyes and used to tell the boys this was because his mother was a Pushtun.

Most Pakistanis have wheat-brown complexions and black or deep brown eyes. Those living in the northern areas of the country are often much fairer and have green or blue eyes. Most of them are ethnic Pushtuns. Various studies have shown that a majority of Pushtuns are the descendants of the marriages between local women and Alexander's soldiers[4] who, before they captured Punjab, had conquered the areas between Taxila and Swat in the north-west of present-day Pakistan.

Musadiq told me that his friends and he had never seen Noor's mother. Noor also had an elder brother and a younger sister, both fair and green-eyed. Noor's father spoke Saraiki.[5] He was brown-skinned, black-eyed and sported a white beard.

Noor, too, spoke Saraiki. One day he told the boys that

he had *Yunani khoon* (Greek blood). When Musadiq asked him how he knew this, he said that his mother had told him. She claimed that thousands of years ago a woman from his mother's tribe in Swat had gotten married to a Greek soldier who had come with Alexander (Sikander). He took her back to Greece where the couple had four children: three boys and a girl. The woman later returned to Swat with the children when the soldier passed away. In Swat, a Greek administrator who had been left behind by Alexander with some soldiers married the widowed woman. She then bore two more children.

Musadiq told me that his friends began to taunt Noor, telling him that the ancient Multani people (Malhi) had defeated Alexander and that he (Alexander) was an idol worshipper. Noor laughed and asked the boys, 'Then who were the Malhi?' Musadiq said that they, being kids, had no clue. They had conveniently assumed that the people of Multan were always Muslim. 'They were Hindus, you fools!' Noor had shot back in Saraiki, implying that they were idol-worshippers too.

Sometime in 1976, Musadiq said, Noor had an argument with his father and told the boys that he was leaving Multan and going to Swat. He said he was going there to stay with his mother's kinfolk and marry a girl from the tribe who had Yunani khoon. Musadiq asked him how he would know she had Greek blood, to which Noor replied, 'Green eyes.'

But that wasn't all. Noor also said that after his marriage, he planned to take his wife to Greece and was going to try and look for their cousins, relatives of the Greek soldier who had come to Swat and returned to Greece. The next day, Noor was gone. A year later, in

1977, the boys suddenly saw him again, sitting outside the tomb and smoking a cigarette. Apparently, he had travelled to Swat and contacted a family belonging to his mother's tribe. He told them about his mother and the whole ancestral history which the males of the family were also familiar with. They treated him well and let him stay in a guest room at their home—that is, until he told an elder male of the family that he was in Swat to marry and wouldn't mind marrying any of his three teenaged (and green-eyed) granddaughters.

This is how Musadiq explained the scene to me: 'Well, Noor told us that the old man quietly nodded his head and politely asked him what he did for a living. Noor said that he was planning to become a homeopath like his father and inherit his father's clinic in Multan. The old man again nodded his head and asked why his father and mother weren't there to talk about his marriage. To this he told the old man that they would, once he told Noor he was willing to get one of his granddaughters married to him. The old man's next question was, "Why your mother didn't marry a Pushtun? Why did she marry a Punjabi?" Noor told him that it was a marriage of convenience brokered by the respective fathers of his parents who were both homeopaths. The old man again nodded his head and after slowly getting up, told him to wait. After a minute or two, the old man returned with a shotgun in his hand! With him were two other male members of the family and all of them gave Noor a sound thrashing ...'

Some three years later, in 1980, Musadiq, who had by then enrolled at the famous National College of Arts in Lahore, bumped into Noor outside the tomb again. Musadiq was visiting Multan during the summer break and had all but forgotten about Noor, who looked haggard and tired. An old school friend of Musadiq's told him that Noor had become a drug addict. The friend said that Noor now lived permanently on the grounds of the tomb and sometimes could be seen begging for alms there. This depressed Musadiq a great deal.

Musadiq asked Noor (in Punjabi), '*Nooray, aye ki hoya?*' (Noor, what's happened to you?). Noor embraced Musadiq and said, '*Ay sab Yunan di tyari ay* ... ' (All this is preparation for Greece). In 1979, Noor had returned to Swat and had started selling baked corn to tourists there. He had set up his small cart very close to the house where he was thrashed. He saw two of the granddaughters get married until he was discovered again by the family and literally chased out of the city. And, indeed, back in Multan he had become hooked to opium. His mother had passed away and his father and siblings had completely disowned him. They believed he had gone insane. Musadiq gave Noor some money and left for Lahore.

Musadiq told me that even though he often went to Multan after completing college, he never saw Noor again. Nor did he ever bother to ask anyone about him. Incidentally, some nine years later, in 1989, when Musadiq met another old schoolmate for lunch in Lahore, the school pal suddenly asked Musadiq whether he had heard about what had happened to Noor.

'Noor?' Musadiq asked, and then remembered, 'Oh, Noor, Yunani khoon?'

'Yes, yes, him,' the friend had replied. 'Did you hear?'

'Hear what?' Musadiq asked.

'He's in Greece.'

Musadiq almost fell off his chair. According to his

friend, Noor had become a very skillful and successful beggar, mostly operating in the vicinity of Rukn-e-Alam's tomb. Apparently, he had collected enough money to get a visa and a plane ticket to Muscat in Oman after he managed to prove that he was the inheritor of his father's clinic. From Muscat he was said to have slipped into Iraq and from Iraq to Turkey and from Turkey into Greece, all illegally. This was confirmed by a school buddy of Musadiq's who claimed to have met and talked to Noor at a supermarket in Muscat in 1987. Noor was working there as a helper at the time.

Musadiq told me that the moment he heard this, he was immediately reminded of what Noor had told him when he last met him outside the tomb in 1980: 'Ay sab Yunan di tyari ay ...'

3

A Dry Run

When I was a child, in the mid-1970s, I once overhead one of my father's friends speaking about a mysterious lake in the Khyber Pakhtunkhwa (KP) province of Pakistan (it was then known as the North-West Frontier Province). Like my father at the time, his friend, too, must have been in his thirties. He spoke of how he planned to find this lake. The lake was called Dhanakosha. I do not remember whether he ever went looking for it, but many years later, I did.

In 1985, I accompanied a group of friends on a road trip from Karachi all the way up to the magnificent Karakoram Highway which connects Pakistan with China. The highway is all of 1,569.5 kilometres from Karachi, the country's southernmost metropolis. We drove in a Toyota four-wheeler across the Sindh province till we arrived in Lahore, the capital of the Punjab province. Here we stayed with the relatives of one of my friends at their lavish bungalow. Much of our time was spent scoring hashish from Lahore's ancient red-light district, the Heera Mandi, and getting high in the washroom of the large guest room we were all lodged in. Then there was a disagreement about something between two of my friends and they stopped talking to each other; so much so that one of them decided to return to Karachi. Well, since I was much closer to him than I was to the others, I decided to take the train back to Karachi with him.

So while the rest of the guys drove on towards the Karakoram, both of us ended up with our backpacks at the Lahore Railway Station. But as we were standing at the ticket counter to buy our tickets for Karachi, my friend noticed that another train, Khyber Mail, was scheduled to leave the station for KP's capital city, Peshawar. In a spur of the moment decision, we decided to travel to Peshawar instead. The plan was to reach Peshawar and then from there hitch a bus ride to the scenic Swat Valley and from Swat, catch another bus to Karakoram and thus travel all the way to the Pak-China border, doing by ourselves by hook or crook what our now-estranged buddies were smoothly doing by car. Between us, we had Rs. 900 which we thought was more than enough to make the spontaneous trip.

We reached Peshawar and stayed at '1 Star Hotel' (that was actually the hotel's name!). Though cheap, it wasn't all that bad. Peshawar at the time was receiving hordes of Afghans coming in through the Khyber Pass due to the civil war in Afghanistan between Soviet-backed Afghan troops and Soviet soldiers on one side and Afghan Islamist groups on the other. The Islamist outfits were being backed by the US, Saudi Arabia and Pakistan. In those days, one could also find quite a few American men and women on the streets of Peshawar, most of them working for the various US-funded organisations helping the Pakistani authorities in propping up the Afghan Islamist groups stationed in

Peshawar, and in aiding the thousands of Afghan refugees who had begun pouring into Peshawar ever since Soviet forces occupied Afghanistan, in December 1979. By the way, my friend and I were self-proclaimed 'Marxists' and weren't sure exactly whom we should support—'our' Soviet Marxist comrades or our own country!

After staying in Peshawar for two days, we took a bus to Swat, which is about 250 kilometres from Peshawar. It is one of KP's most picturesque regions and a tourist magnet. Or at least it used to be till a vicious war erupted here between Islamic extremists and the Pakistan army many years later, in 2009. The celebrated and brave educationist, Malala Yousufzai, is from Swat. But she wasn't even born yet when my friend and I reached Swat in April 1986. The weather was nice and balmy. We moved into a tourist guest house which seemed to be made entirely from wood. In the afternoon we strolled out to have lunch. The streets were packed with locals and tourists from within Pakistan and abroad. Our plan was to stay in Swat for two days then take a bus to the Pak-China border before returning to Peshawar (also by bus) and catch a train back to Karachi.

We sat outside a roadside eatery for lunch and ordered some *anda-channa*[1] and colas. On a table near ours were three men, two of them middle-aged Chinese and their Pushtun tour guide. They had a map which lay open in front of them. They were all talking in whatever little English they knew. I did not pay much attention until about fifteen minutes later I heard the word Dhanakosha. I turned to look and heard it again, uttered by one of the Chinese.

'They are looking for Dhanakosha,' I told my friend.

'What's Dhanakosha?' he asked.

'I don't know,' I replied. 'It's some mysterious lake.'

'So?' My friend replied. 'Why are you so interested?'

With a hand gesture I asked him to wait and turned my chair to face the three men. 'Excuse me,' I said, very politely. They all stopped talking and turned their heads towards me.

'Hello,' one of the Chinese smiled.

'Are you looking for Dhanakosha?' I asked.

'Are you looking for it too?' the Chinese inquired.

'No, but I was just curious about it. It is called the mysterious lake. Why is that?' I queried.

'No, no,' he replied, 'No mysterious; very holy,' he said.

'It's a holy lake?' I asked.

This question was answered by the young guide, 'Sir, it is holy for them. Where are you from? Lahore?'

'Karachi,' I said. Then turning back to the Chinese, I asked, 'Dhanakosha is holy for the Chinese?'

This made both the Chinese men laugh. Then one of them said: 'No, no. No Chinese. Tibet. You know Tibet?'

They weren't Chinese but Tibetans. 'Yes,' I said. 'I know Tibet. Beautiful place, but part of China, no?'

'No, no, China occupy Tibet. Tibet want free,' one of the Tibetans replied, now almost frowning.

I swiftly changed the topic back to Dhanakosha. 'So why is Dhanakosha holy for Tibetans?'

One of them got up and moved towards our table with his chair. He placed the chair at our table and then turned to pick up the map. I slightly moved my plate of anda-chana so he could place the map on the table between himself and me. Then he put a finger on a point on the map which was showing an area between Swat and

Lower Dir: 'You see here? Here was lake. Dhanakosha. Many years old. Now no lake.'

I nodded my head, as my friend continued to eat his lunch. 'But why holy lake?' I asked.

'Our prophet born there,' he replied, smiling.

'In Lower Dir?'

'Yes, many hundred year ago,' he said. 'Padmasambhava.'

I had never heard of him. Or her. So I apologetically shrugged my shoulders.

He laughed, 'It's alright. But you hear of Buddha?'

'Yes. Of course,' I replied.

'Padmasambhava is Buddha prophet.' Clearly, what he wanted to say was that this Padmasambhava was a Buddhist prophet.

'When was he born?' I asked.

'Many years,' he said. 'Eighth century.'

He then explained that Padmasambhava was born (thirteen hundred years ago) in an area which today lies somewhere between Swat and Lower Dir in present-day Pakistan. This region at the time was under the Oddiyyana dynasty[2] which was Buddhist.

'He (Padmasambhava) born in Dhanakosha,' he told me.

'He was born near the lake?' I asked.

'Yes, on big leaf floating on lake,' he explained.

'Really?' I half-smiled, exhibiting a bit of scepticism.

I knew that many parts which are today in Pakistan had Buddhist kingdoms till the eighth century, but somehow I had never heard of Padmasambhava. The Tibetan didn't say much else apart from the fact that Padmasambhava was the one who had travelled to Tibet and introduced Buddhism in that region. Today that strand of the faith is called 'Tibetan Buddhism'.

I thought I just had to visit the area that the Tibetan had pointed out on the map. It was very close to Swat. So I told my friend that we should go there instead of the Pak-China border. He refused. In fact, he now wanted to return to Karachi. I told him that since I had accompanied him instead of driving towards the Karakoram with the other guys, he was obliged to return the favour. He grumbled a bit but then agreed to come with me. The area where, according to the Tibetan, the lake once was, is called Chakdara.

Chakdara is a village near Lower Dir. It is about a five-hour drive from Swat and that's exactly how much time it took for a bus to drop us there. And indeed, the place was sprawling with ancient Buddhist sites. Unfortunately, there were no guides there, though there was a tiny museum which had Buddhist artifacts from the Gandhara period. This period lasted from the first millennium BCE till the eighth century CE[4] in what today lies north of Pakistan and in Afghanistan. Much of this period in these areas was dominated by Buddhist dynasties. In the tiny museum I bought a thin booklet which had brief essays on the Gandhara period. One essay was by the famous Pakistani archaeologist and historian Ahmad Hasan Dani. This essay I found most interesting because it mentioned both Padmasambhava and Dhanakosha.

The only attendant at the museum was a young, bored Pushtun. After I managed to engage him about the subject of the lake, he did indicate that the people of the area were aware about an ancient 'miraculous spring' which sprang up and 'gave birth to a boy' who grew up and become a Buddhist holy man. I asked him where that lake/spring was and he told me it was in what today is the Uchh village some seven kilometres north of Chakdara. While my friend stayed behind (trying to score some hashish), I took a rickshaw to the site of the elusive lake.

Indeed, the area was an important Buddhist site, as noted by the booklet. The rickshaw driver knew about the lake. He took me to a spot which lay just outside the village. It was bone-dry and covered with shrubs. 'This is where the spring was,' he told me. It was as if here the ground had been shaped hundreds of years ago by running water. I paid the rickshaw man and descended into the dry, shallow depression which was certainly a lake or a river once. The weather was partly cloudy and a strong breeze was blowing. I sat on this ancient ground and began to read Dani's essay.

Dani had excavated a first century Buddhist monastery here in 1962. About the lake, he wrote that it is repeatedly mentioned in ancient Tibetan Buddhist texts as the birthplace of Padmasambhava. Many archaeologists (including Dani) went looking for it. Some believe it was a spring situated exactly at the spot where I sat reading Dani's essay. Some believe it still exists and is called Lake Godur situated on a tall mountain in the present-day north Pakistan area of Kalam. But Dani added that the greater likelihood was that the lake/spring once ran in an area between Swat and Lower Dir. This is what the two Tibetans who I had met in Swat also believed.

On Padmasambhava, Dani wrote that he was born in this area in the eighth century CE. Ancient Tibetan Buddhist sources claim that his birth took place 'on a lotus leaf which was floating on Lake Dhanakosha'. When Padmasambhava began to preach, people of the area saw him as a reincarnation of Gautama Buddha. This included a local Oddiyyana king in Swat. The king offered him to take his place on the throne but Padmasambhava refused and instead became a roving Buddhist missionary.

As he moved out and reached areas which are today in India, his reputation grew until he reached Tibet (travelling from present-day Nepal). There his teachings evolved and a strand of Buddhism called Tibetan Buddhism arose which is still the majority-faith in Tibet. Not much else is known about the historical Padmasambhava, even though various myths about his divinity arose in Tibet and South Asia from the ninth century CE. Historians and archaeologists agree that a Buddhist monk who was indeed born during the rule of an eighth century Buddhist dynasty in what today is an area between Swat and Lower Dir, did travel to Tibet and introduce Buddhism there.

After sitting for over an hour on what many claim is the dry bed of the ancient lake Dhanakosha, I took a rickshaw back to Chakdara. I found my friend sitting under a tree playing with two goats. He was feeding them leaves. He looked bored.

'You couldn't get any?' I asked, laughing. I was referring to the hashish he was trying to score.

'Fuck that,' he said. 'Did you find your lake?'

'Actually I did,' I said. 'No better high than that,' I taunted him.

'Fuck that,' he frowned. 'Let's get out of this graveyard.'

'Yes,' I replied. 'I was thinking ...'

He interrupted: 'Yes, me too. Let's go to Peshawar, score some hashish, and then right away take a train back to Karachi.'

'No,' I said. 'I was actually thinking of moving further up.'

'Karakoram?' he asked, looking surprised.

'Further up,' I said, smiling.

'*Behenchodh*, cut out the riddles,' he said, irritated. 'My *bacchhi* (girlfriend) hasn't heard from me in days. And your bacchhi doesn't seem to care.' Fact was, my bacchhi had actually broken off the relationship just before I headed for Lahore. She thought I listened more attentively to Pink Floyd and Aziz Mian Qawwal than I did to her. True.

Anyway, my friend asked me what I had meant by going further up.

'Tibet,' I replied. 'Let's go to Tibet.'

'Have you lost your mind?' my friend almost shouted. Then picking up his backpack, he said he was off to take a bus to Peshawar. 'They will lock you up in China even before you reach Tibet, idiot!' he shouted as he began to walk away. Clearly, he didn't know his geography or recent history. I hadn't either till the Tibetans had recently given me a short lesson. But, that's another matter.

'But I am a Marxist!' I shouted back.

'You are a Buddhist anarchist now, asshole!' he bellowed.

I burst out laughing and ran to join him. By midnight, we were in Peshawar. We spent the whole night on the platform of the city's railway station before taking the train to Karachi at about six in the morning. We couldn't score any hashish. And this depressed my friend. On the train, as he was about to drift into sleep, I said: 'I tell you, buddy, you should have been there. Sitting in that dry lake was the best high.'

'Yes,' he mumbled, about to fall asleep. 'I'm sure it was. I should have left you there ... asshole.'

4

My Name Is Pakistan and I'm Not an Arab

Ever since the early 1970s, the Jamaat-i-Islami (JI), one of Pakistan's oldest Islamic political parties, frequently organises what it calls 'Yaum Babul Islam' (Babul Islam means the 'harbinger of Islam' in Sindhi). It is an event celebrating the conquest of Sindh by Arab commander Mohammad-bin-Qasim (in the eighth century CE) and it is commemorated as 'the advent of Islam in South Asia'. Speakers at this event often describe Qasim as the 'first Pakistani' and then trace and place the creation of Pakistan to the arrival of the Arab commander 1,300 years ago.

Curiously, the JI was originally opposed to the man who actually created Pakistan (in 1947): Mohammad Ali Jinnah.[1] JI's founder, Abul Ala Maududi, had found Jinnah to be steeped in what he called the 'Western notion' of nationalism and too Westernised to deliver and head a Muslim state. So what is one to make of the whole idea of an ancient Arab commander being posthumously raised to become the main architect of what hundreds of years later would become Pakistan? Should one see it as something in tune with JI's Arab-centric concept of Pakistani nationhood? Or is it something else, really?

For starters, it is important to understand that it wasn't really the JI that had first initiated the idea of propping up an eighth century Arab as the true founder of Pakistan. This impression which, from the late 1970s onwards, has found ample space in the country's school text books, was first alluded to in a 1953 book, *Five Years of Pakistan*. The book was published by the government to commemorate the fifth anniversary of Pakistan and in one of its chapters authored by archaeologists associated with a state-funded archaeology project, the authors described Sindh (after it was invaded by Qasim) 'as the first Islamic province in South Asia'.

Even though allusions to Qasim being the 'first Pakistani' can be found in various publications after 1953, he was first officially adopted as the 'first citizen of Pakistan' in *Fifty Years of Pakistan* published by the Federal Bureau of Pakistan in 1998.[2] Nevertheless, as stated previously, the whole notion of Qasim's invasion of Sindh being the genesis of a separate Muslim state in South Asia was first imagined by a handful of Pakistani archaeologists in 1953. It then found its way into the narrative of religious parties such as the JI, before percolating into school text books after the severe existential crisis that the country faced when its eastern wing (the former East Pakistan) broke away in December 1971 to become Bangladesh. In a manner of speaking, this lionisation of Qasim meant that the 'real Pakistan' had always existed in the West, along the Indus (and not in the East).

The notion was then aggressively promoted by the reactionary Zia-ul-Haq dictatorship (1977-1988). It sought to 'explain' Pakistan as a nation that had deep roots in the ancient deserts of Arabia though its geographical location was in the congested expanses of South Asia. What's even more puzzling is the fact that as far as South Asian history is concerned, or even in the history of the Arabs, Qasim's foray into Sindh was much ado about nothing. It was by no stretch of imagination the significant event it is made out to be.

There is a silence which typically greets historians when they go looking for ancient sources about the event. There are almost none. This gives rise to the question: if Qasim's invasion of Sindh was such a grand undertaking, why is it only scarcely mentioned in the available sources from that period? The earliest available source to mention the invasion is the ninth century book *Kitab Futuh al-Buldan* by Arab historian al-Baladhuri. It was written more than a hundred years after the invasion. Then there is also the thirteenth century Persian text called *Chachnama* that was authored almost 400 years after Qasim's forces arrived on the shores of Sindh.

When historians piece together whatever little early sources there are about the event, it transpires that the Arabs had first begun to exhibit interest in Sindh in 634 CE. The Umayyads (the first major Muslim empire) sent troops to conquer Sindh on a number of occasions between 644 CE and 710 CE. Most of these raids were repulsed by local tribes, even though at times Arab armies did manage to hold on to Makran (south of Sindh) for brief periods of time. The reasons for the Umayyads to enter the region were mainly two: it was a rapidly expanding empire and wanted to get a toehold in the region, and it wanted to gain control of the region's lucrative port trade.

The popular narrative found in most post ninth century Muslim history books about Qasim's invasion portrays him as being sent to Sindh by the Umayyad governor in Baghdad to avenge the plundering of Arab ships by Sindh's pirates and the refusal of Sindh's ruler, Raja Dahir, to do anything about it. Historians such as Dr Mubarak Ali and Prof. Manan Ahmed Asif, who have tried to substantiate this narrative with the help of the existing ancient sources, have found only sketchy evidence.

Manan concluded, 'Qasim's expedition was merely the latest in a sixty-year long campaign by Arab regimes to gain a foothold over the port trades and to extract riches from these port communities (in Sindh and Makran).'[3] Qasim's supposedly Islamic genesis-like manoeuvres in Sindh are largely a myth. In 731 CE when al-Hakim al-Kalbi was appointed governor of Sindh (some twenty years after Qasim's death), he found a land where a majority of those who had converted to Islam (during Qasim's stay there) had reverted back to being either Hindu or Buddhist.[4]

The question now is: if Qasim's invasion was comparatively a minor historical event, how did it become so exaggerated? We have already seen how and why it gained such existential significance in Pakistan. But it remained almost forgotten for hundreds of years, even during much of the 500-year-long Muslim rule in India. Interest in Qasim was ironically reignited by British colonialists in the nineteenth century.[5] British author James Mill, in his book *The History of British India* (1817), talks of Qasim as an invader who created a rupture in the region. He presents very little evidence but his lead was followed by other British authors of the era who all saw Qasim as the man who opened the gates for hordes of Muslim invaders to pour in and destroy the Indian civilization.

This narrative of a bloodletting Qasim was then picked up by early Hindu nationalists who had otherwise largely forgotten about this eighth century Arab. A couple of nineteenth century Muslim historians, such as Syed Suleman Nadvi and Mohammad Hanif, responded by offering a more studied look at Qasim's invasion, describing it as nothing like the one that was being peddled by the British colonialists and early Hindu nationalists.

Nadvi and Hanif portrayed Qasim as a just, tolerant and gallant man. Both these versions of the man emerged from the highly polemical debate on Qasim's invasion which erupted in the nineteenth century between the British, Hindu and Muslim historians. The truth is, to 'neutral' history, Qasim remains a figure about whom sources say very little. But ever since the nineteenth century, he has been at the heart of an overtly glorious myth to some, and an equally mythical force of destruction to others. The truth probably lies somewhere in the middle.

In 1984, Anwar Qureshi AKA *Punter*, one of the first friends that I made at a college in Karachi, related to me a rather interesting episode from his childhood. Qureshi was a very shy and reserved seventeen-year-old when I first met him, in 1983. But for some reason he did often allow himself to open up a bit when with me.

Anwar belonged to a middle-class Sindhi family settled in Karachi, but the family originally hailed from Sukkur, a town approximately 750 kilometres from Karachi. Once, in the college's canteen, Anwar told me that back in 1974 when he was a Grade III student at a public school in Sukkur, he was told by a teacher that Mohammad-bin-Qasim was one of the founders of Pakistan.

He repeated this in front of his father at home and the father immediately asked him who had told him this. Anwar's father had been in high school when Pakistan came into being in August 1947; he was also a passionate member of the All India Muslim Students' Federation (AIMSF), the student-wing of Jinnah's centrist All India Muslim League (AIML). Even though the father was disappointed by the party's performance after Pakistan's creation, and by the late 1960s had become a fan of Sindhi nationalist ideologue and scholar, G. M. Syed, this couldn't curtail his anger when his son told him that it was a teacher at school who had called Qasim a founder of Pakistan.

'It was Mohammad Ali Jinnah!' his father had shot back. 'What Qasim?'

After enquiring the name of the teacher (Khalid), the father almost immediately jumped onto his motorbike and rode towards the school with Anwar placed firmly on the backseat of the bike. By the time they reached the school, the teacher had already left and gone home. So off they went to meet the teacher at his residence which was not very far away. The father banged at his door, drawing the teacher out.

'What's the matter, Sir?' asked the teacher (in Sindhi), recognising that it was Anwar's father. 'Is everything alright?'

'No!' bellowed the father. 'Why are you screwing up your students' heads with fantasies?'

'Sir, what did I do?' the surprised teacher asked.

'You told my son Mohammad-bin-Qasim was a founder of Pakistan? Where did this stupid Arab come in from?' the father shouted.

The teacher relaxed a bit and asked the father to do

the same: 'Sir, it is not my fault. We teach students about Jinnah. But now we have to take Qasim's name too.' He took Anwar and his father inside his house and showed the father a history book that had been issued for the students of Grades III, IV and V by the government of Pakistan. And indeed, somewhere in the book, Qasim was hailed as 'one of the early founders of (what would become) Pakistan'.

What's even funnier was when Anwar told me that in a history test (in Grade IV) he described Qasim exactly the way he had heard his father describe him that day. Anwar said: 'I wrote, "Qasim was an Arab fool".' Apparently, Anwar had no idea what a 'fool' was. He thought it was another word for soldier.

I kept bumping into Anwar off and on after college till he got married in 2000 and, later, moved to Canada. He had become a chartered accountant by then. After many years, I bumped into him again in February 2017 at the Karachi Literature Festival (KLF). I was at the event to launch my second book, *The Pakistan Anti-Hero*, and spotted him in the audience. He met me after the session. He was there with his wife (Sumbul) and his two sons (nine-year-old Rehan and four-year-old Azan). I invited them for some coffee at a make-shift café. Here, while signing a copy of my book for him, I asked, 'So, Punter, how is your relationship with Qasim these days?'

Hearing me say this, Anwar burst out laughing, 'I still think he is an Arab fool.' And then hastily added, 'But I make sure my children describe him as a founder (of Pakistan) in their school exams.'*

---

*His wife and children hadn't yet joined him in Canada when I met him.

5

Dubious Ancestors

In 1981, a book arrived in the offices of my paternal grandfather. It was authored by a distant cousin of his and a fellow Paracha. It was called the *History & Culture of the Paracha Tribe*. Originally penned in Urdu, among other things, it claimed that the Paracha tribe were descendants of a man called Ali Yemeni from Arabia, who had converted to Islam during the early days of the faith in the seventh century CE.

The book went on to suggest that the tribe followed Yemeni into Persia where the Parachas became traders. From Persia, various branches of the tribe spread out across north India, Central Asia and Afghanistan. I was only fourteen when this book was published. It was rather nice to know that the tribe that I belonged to had not only been Muslim for hundreds of years, but also had Arab genes. The author of the book had not cited any convincing sources to substantiate his claim other than mentioning what he had heard from his immediate elders. But his narrative about the origins of the Paracha clan became rather popular among Paracha brethren in Pakistan.

Even though as a teen I, too, had believed the claims

made in the book, these claims began to come apart when, as a college student in the mid and late 1980s, I came across a few tomes which challenged the contents of the history textbooks being taught in Pakistan's educational institutions. It was a liberating feeling. What pioneering Pakistani 'revisionist historians'[1] such as Dr Mubarak Ali, K. K. Aziz and Ayesha Jalal also did for young folk like me was to inform us how one ought to go about authenticating (or rejecting) claims presented as historical facts.

Surely, I thought, there must be more about the Paracha tribe beyond verbal folklore and modern narratives woven to suit contemporary theological, social and political trends. One had to of course, look for it. I tucked this thought away in the back of my mind as a possible future project.

In early 1993, I was a reporter for an English weekly and happened to be in Islamabad covering Benazir Bhutto's 'long march' against the first Nawaz Sharif regime when I stumbled upon a dusty old book called *Tribes & Castes of Punjab and NWFP* at a tiny bookstore in Islamabad. The book had been published in the early 1900s and was authored by H. Arthur Rose, a British bureaucrat serving in the British colonial government in India.

It turned out to be a fascinating read. Based entirely on two detailed reports on the census conducted by the colonial set-up in Punjab and the North-West Frontier Province (NWFP) in 1883 and 1892, there was a whole section on the Paracha tribe in it. According to the report, the Parachas mostly resided in the hilly Potohar region of north Punjab and in areas near the Punjab-NWFP border. In fact, they still do. Most fascinating (at least to me) was when the 1883 census report reproduced in the book quoted some elders of the tribe saying that the

Paracha tribe had migrated from Persia as Zoroastrians and became Buddhists in India. They then converted to Islam sometime in the twelfth century CE.

But just as the dubious 1981 book had done, the nineteenth century census reports too were quoting Paracha elders. Nevertheless, another book confirmed what the nineteenth century Paracha elders were suggesting. In his hefty 2007 book, *Pakistan Through the Ages,* famous Pakistani archaeologist, historian and linguist Ahmad Hasan Dani mentions the names of some of the tribes who had accompanied the Kushan people into areas that today fall in Pakistan. The Kushans had established an empire in Afghanistan and north-western Pakistan between first and third centuries CE.

According to Dani's archaeological findings, the Kushans were a syncretic people in Persia and Central Asia. They were followers of a faith that was a hybrid of Zoroastrianism and classical Greek mythology. During the time of the empire's greatest ruler, Kanishka, the empire became entirely Buddhist. One of the tribes, which Dani suggests accompanied the Kushans into today's Pakistan, was called Pirache which later became Paracha (sometimes Piracha). So there it was, the true history of my people.

I think I'd rather stick to the claims of an accomplished archaeologist and historian than some guy who concocted a figure called Ali Yemeni because he found the idea of being from Arabia rather appealing. Anyway, these days a simple DNA tracking method can actually trace back one's ancestors millions of years. Take the example of the Pakistani-American lad who was always told that his ancestors came from Arabia. Then in August 2016 he got his DNA tested. The results showed that he was 97 per cent South Asian and had zero per cent Middle Eastern ancestry. He gleefully announced these results in a video on YouTube.[2]

Dr Mubarak Ali, in his book *In Search of Identity*[3] writes that the practice of claiming non-South-Asian ancestry among the region's Muslims began during the collapse of the Mughal Empire in the eighteenth century CE. According to him, the Mughals largely employed Persian-speaking men in their courts. Almost all of them were migrants from Persia or Central Asia. But when the influence and power of the Mughal dynasty began to recede, such men stopped coming to India. Their places were gradually filled by 'local converts' or South Asian men who had converted to Islam (from Hinduism, Buddhism, Zoroastrianism and other religions in the region).

The resultant ascent of local Muslims in India initially saw them taken pride in their 'local' roots (thus the sudden mushrooming of Urdu). But Dr Ali suggests that once they were established as the new courtiers, traders, feudal lords and members of an expanding Muslim middle-class in India, most of them began to alter their ancestral histories. Since the idea of nobility was still associated with non-South-Asian Muslims, and the fact that Muslims of India had begun to see themselves as a separate cultural entity, claiming to have origins outside of South Asia became the norm.

This norm continued even after the creation of Pakistan—especially from the mid-1970s onward when, because of the rise of oil-rich monarchies in the Middle East and the growth of so-called political Islam[4]—the trend of claiming Arabian ancestry became rampant. But the thing is, the many social and political complexities of this issue can now actually be untangled in one go by 'Human Mitochondrial DNA (mtDNA) testing'. It is simple and relatively cheap. Apparently, a person can get one done for less than 150 dollars.

In 1987, three well-known genealogists (Cann, Stoneking and Wilson) published a stunning report of a worldwide mtDNA survey.[5] The survey had collected DNA samples of numerous men and women from around the world to see who originated where. As they dug deeper and looked further back, they discovered that mtDNA in every living person on the planet today goes back to a woman who lived in Africa some 200,000 years ago! Scientists now believe that no matter what faith, language, nationality, immediate ancestral history or colour of skin one possesses, he or she came from that woman who was a member of a pre-historic tribe in Africa. A rather humbling thought.

6

A Saint's Journey

In early 1984, when I was a student at college, I made a trip to India (my first and last). My fellow travellers on that trip were three Sindhi-speaking friends. We went to Mumbai (then called Bombay) first and then to Pune (then called Poona) and Goa, staying in low-rent hotels everywhere. This inspite of the fact that one of my Sindhi friends had some distant relatives in Mumbai.

Later, it turned out that the relatives were not relatives at all. To begin with, they were Hindu. They had been neighbours of the friend's family in what is today Sukkur in Pakistan and had migrated to India in March 1948, almost a year after Pakistan's creation. We visited their apartment at the tail-end of our trip. In their drawing room was a huge painting of a bearded man sitting on a lotus flower in the middle of a river surrounded by a school of fish that seemed to be swimming in a circle around him.

I asked the family about the image. They told me that the man was Jhuley Lal, the patron saint of Sindhi Hindus. They claimed that every Sindhi home in India had a picture of him. Two years later, I was travelling in the interior of Pakistan's Sindh province with another group of friends. We were all members of a progressive student outfit at our college. Our plan was to drive up to the town of Dadu and try to meet Sindhi nationalist scholar G. M. Syed, who was reported to be under house arrest there.

Though I was opposed to Syed's political dimension of Sindhi nationalism,[1] I was, nevertheless, a great admirer of his scholarly work, especially of his book *Religion and Reality* in which he had painstakingly charted the centuries-old evolution of Sufism in the Sindh region. I believe he did mention Jhuley Lal in passing in his book, but I wasn't sure because I had read it in 1983 during my first year in college. (No, it wasn't part of the curriculum!)

Our group of activists was unable to meet Syed since he was not in Dadu. On our way back to Karachi, we stopped at a rickety eatery in a village in the Sanghar district. As we entered the place for a cup of tea and some cigarettes, the first thing I noticed on the mud wall was a poster ... of Jhuley Lal! I had forgotten about him. But it was the same image I had first come across in the Bombay home. A man with a flowing white beard, sitting on a lotus flower in the middle of a river and surrounded by silver-coloured fish.

But there was one difference. In the image of his that I had seen in Bombay, he was holding a rosary whose beads had tiny inscriptions carved in the Sanskrit language. But in the poster at the eatery, he was holding and reading the Muslim holy book: the Quran. Intrigued, I asked a Sindhi friend of mine in the group who the man was. '*Arré Paracha Sain, tum ko nahi pata? Yeh Baba Sheikh Tahir hai...*' (You don't know? He is Baba Sheikh Tahir).

I told him that I had seen an image of him in the

home of a Sindhi Hindu family in India and that they had called him Jhuley Lal. The friend began to laugh at my confusion. He then drove me some fifty kilometres north of the village to a small, dusty town called Udero Lal. In this town, he took me to a beautiful and spacious white shrine with prominent domes. This is where Sheikh Tahir was buried, I was told. He then made me meet one of the keepers of the shrine who was a Sindhi and could not speak any Urdu. But strangely, he spoke Punjabi fluently!

He told me that the shrine had been constructed in the seventeenth century—1684 CE to be precise—according to Din Mohammad Vai's *Tazkirah-i-Mashahir-i-Sindh*. The keeper claimed that Sheikh Tahir was born a Hindu but converted to Islam as a teen. His Hindu name had been Udero Lal. The shrine was frequented by Muslims as well as the Hindus of Sindh. The group of keepers that look after the shrine also included Hindus.

Another fascinating aspect of the shrine was a small room that housed a steadily burning flame. The flame has supposedly been kept burning by generations of keepers for over 400 years now. The keeper didn't know exactly why. The keeper informed me, 'Udero Lal was an upright man with a strong strain of spirituality. It was because of him that the Hindus of Sindh were different and did not practise the caste system...'

This seems to be correct. The famous nineteenth century British traveller, Richard Francis Burton, in his writings written during his long stay in Sindh in the mid-1800s, wrote: 'Hinduism in Sindh is mixed and has adopted many aspects of Islam and Sikhism. The Hindus (of Sindh) often become followers of Muslim saints here ...'[2]

Impressed by Lal's spiritual disposition and work

against the caste system, a Muslim Sufi saint from Multan is said to have converted him to Islam. 'This is when Udero Lal became Sheikh Tahir,' the keeper had told me. He said despite this, Hindus of the area continued to revere him, and so did thousands of Lal's Muslim devotees. On our way back to Sanghar, I asked my friend why Sheikh Tahir continues to sit on a lotus flower in the middle of a river in all of his images.

The friend responded by saying that Hindus of Sindh believed that Lal had 'emerged' from the river Indus. He added that the Muslims began to believe the tale when they saw *palla* fish (indigenous to river Indus) circling a small shrine of Lal which is located on an island in the middle of the river near the city of Bhakkar (in southern Punjab).

Interestingly, in Bhakkar, Jhuley Lal is called Khwaja Khizar. In 1991, while editing an article written (on the Bhakkar shrine) by a French anthropologist for the English weekly I worked for, I learned that, indeed, schools of the palla fish did go around in circles around the tiny island. But he added that this was due to the mating and feeding cycle of the fish. So, in a way, ancient Muslims and Hindus of the region were explaining a purely natural phenomenon through mystical imagery.

Jhuley Lal is not as major a Sufi saint in Sindh as are the great Shah Latif or the revered Lal Shahbaz. Yet, it was Jhuley Lal who ended up on the walls of Sindhi-speakers in India. I've always wondered why. This inquiry of mine finally came full circle when I discovered a book entitled *Interpreting the Sindh World*[3] in 2015.

In an essay (in the book) on the saint, Lata Parwani suggests that when Sindhi Hindus migrated to India during

Partition in 1947, they felt spiritually alienated because they could not relate to the forms of Hinduism that were practised there. Noticing this, one Professor Ram Panjwani, a Sindhi educationist, began a movement among the Sindhi Hindus in India to revitalise Jhuley Lal as their main deity. He succeeded, and to this day most Sindhi Hindus in India revere a saint that their elders had brought from Sindh, which became part of Muslim-majority Pakistan in 1947.

7

A Matter of Land

As a child and then as a teen, I loved visiting the fruit and sugarcane farms belonging to a maternal uncle of my father's. The farms were located in the rural outskirts of the small southern Punjab city of Sadiqabad, some 625 kilometres from Karachi where I lived. Even though our family and the Paracha clan hail from the northern-most parts of the Punjab, this uncle had bought land in the deep south of the province.

I would often spend weeks on the farm during my winter vacations. I last stayed there in January 1983 after which the uncle sold his land holdings and moved to Karachi. I was sixteen at the time and thus able to move around his vast fertile domains on my own. Once during this visit when I was playing cricket with my uncle's two sons on a dirt road near the farms, I saw a peasant arguing (in Saraiki) with a cop. The sons rushed to the site of the argument because the peasant was their father's employee.

The peasant was accusing the cop of asking him for 'more bribe'. The cop, a junior officer at a police station (*thana*) in the village, used to extort money from peasants and petty farmers to 'keep their daughters safe from being picked up by lecherous feudal lords'. One of the uncle's sons told me that a year ago a relative of a feudal lord had attempted to kidnap a peasant's daughter. But despite the fact that he was arrested and jailed, the cop used the event to instill fear in the hapless peasants, telling them that he alone stood between the feudal lords and their daughters.

During the argument I noticed that the peasant kept saying (to the cop), '*Tu Tulgaki ho gaya hai...*' (You have become *Tulgaki*). I asked one of the uncle's sons what Tulgaki was because I had never heard the term before. It wasn't Urdu and it wasn't Punjabi, so maybe it was Saraiki? Not quite. Because the same day my uncle told me that by Tulgaki the peasant had meant *Tughlaqi*. I had never heard that one before either, so the uncle elaborated (in Punjabi), 'Tughlaqi means behaving like Muhammad-bin-Tughlaq.'

Muhammad-bin-Tughlaq was a fourteenth century king (Sultan) who was part of the Delhi Sultanate. The Sultanate was mostly made up of Muslim dynasties which ruled large parts of the subcontinent from 1206 CE to 1526 CE. Three of these dynasties were made up of Turkic Muslims who had invaded India from their homelands in Central Asia. The Tughlaq dynasty (1321-1351 CE) was one of the three Turkic dynasties of the Sultanate and Muhammad-bin-Tughlaq was the dynasty's second Sultan and perhaps its most controversial monarch.

A highly educated man who was proficient in Greek logic, mathematics, astronomy, philosophy, medicine, religion, and Persian and Arabic literature, historians also often describe Muhammad-bin-Tughlaq as impulsive, high-strung, moody and 'eccentric'.[1] At times, he was even called 'the mad king'.[2] Some now believe he was a genius who was ahead of his time and thus misunderstood.[3] He introduced certain economic, land and military reforms which in the future came to be accepted as modern and rational but in fourteenth century India, they were seen as being foolish and even 'insane'.

But why was a twentieth century Saraiki peasant in Pakistan uttering the name of a medieval Turkic sultan who had ruled the region from Delhi and for some time from Daulatabad in what is today the Maharashtra state in India? According to my uncle, the peasant's ancestors were not originally Saraiki nor were they from the land on which they now toiled. According to him, they were a community of peasants in the area whose ancestors were from the Doab region near the Ganges and Yamuna rivers in what is today India.

Apparently, the ancestors of this community had been petty farmers and peasants who had converted to Islam (from Hinduism) at the beginning of the rule of the Delhi Sultanate in the early thirteenth century CE. When Muhammad-bin-Tughlaq began levying heavy taxes on the Doab's farmers and peasants during a famine, they rose up in revolt. Even though Tughlaq quickly realised his mistake and began to actually help the affected peasants, most of them continued to rebel. Many became outlaws and some migrated from Doab to other areas.[4]

About two thousand peasants (all Muslim converts) migrated to areas which today are in Pakistan's Punjab province. Many then travelled further down and settled as peasants in Sadiqabad. Over the next six hundred years, this community adopted the language and traditions of southern Punjab's Saraiki region.

There was very little that they now retained of the culture of their Doab ancestors. Except the word Tulgaki which was most probably coined by their ancestors in the Doab during Tughlaq's taxation drive hundreds of years ago. As a word it had come to mean an oppressor, exploiter and/or an extortionist. That's what the peasant was calling the cop. Many years later, in the late 1990s, while talking to the sons of the uncle, I, for reasons which I now fail to recall, brought up the episode of the peasant and the cop which we had witnessed back in 1983. One of the sons immediately replied (in Punjabi): 'The peasant's family became Tulgaki as well!'

According to him, when his father (the uncle) sold all his land holdings in the mid-1980s, the new landlord who was one of the few rich members of the Doab community, gifted the peasant a tiny plot of land. The peasant sold the land and moved his family to Lahore. There he set up a small vegetable shop and sent his son (but not his two daughters) to a government school. The son had been studying at a seminary in the village before the family moved to Lahore. The peasant made enough money to expand his shop and set up another one in the same area of Lahore. He also sent his son to college. In 1992, when the son received his Bachelor's degree, he convinced his father to let him sell one of the two shops (so he could start his own business). The father agreed.

The son sold the shop and moved back to Sadiqabad. There he bought a small plot of agriculture land. He grew fruit (mostly oranges) on his piece of land. He eventually landed a deal with a local juice-making company and supplied them with the fruit he grew. The company distributed its brand of fruit juices only in Sadiqabad and the adjoining Rahim Yar Khan.

By 1995, the son had made enough money to buy a larger plot of land. So much so that in early 1997 he asked a political party (I don't recall which one) to give him a ticket for that year's Punjab Assembly election. He actually got a ticket after convincing the party that he would be able to attract the votes of his community of Saraikis. As it turns out, he lost the election badly.

This is how it happened. After he had bought the new piece of land in 1995, he got a business partner of his (a petty feudal) to forcibly evacuate four peasant families who were living in their mud huts on that plot. He wanted to grow sugarcane there and thought that the peasants were sitting on a particularly fertile patch. What he didn't know was that after this forcible evacuation, the peasants of the area had all begun to call him Tulgaki.

And as one of the sons of the uncle concluded: 'Now why would anyone want to vote for a Tulgaki, right?'

8

The Minister of the Kitchen

The Burns Road locality in Karachi is an extremely crowded and polluted area today. Until the late 1950s it used to be a 'posh' locality where the city's wealthy and middle-class Hindus and Muslims had their bungalows, apartments and shops. Developed by British colonialists in the early 1900s and named after an eighteenth century British 'spy-doctor' who had worked for the British Raj in North India,[1] Burns Road was a locality in Karachi where sections of the first major wave of Urdu-speaking Muslim migrants had settled after the creation of Pakistan, in 1947.

A majority of these refugees came from the towns and cities of North India. The lucky ones managed to occupy the homes and shops here that were vacated by the Hindus who departed for India. This happened inspite of the fact that Karachi had remained largely peaceful during the deadly communal riots and clashes involving Hindus, Sikhs and Muslims of British India on the eve of the India-Pakistan Partition.[2] But it took just one major riot in Karachi's Guru Mandir area in January 1948[3] to trigger a mass exodus of Hindus from the city who till 1947 had constituted 51 per cent of Karachi's population.[4]

By the 1960s Burns Road had become a chaotic and congested locality, but it had gained fame for its dingy cafes, eateries and bakeries dishing out the most delicious food and bakery items made from the recipes and cooking expertise brought here by the North Indian Muslim migrants who came post 1947. Most of these dishes were traditional *Mughaliana* items, or cuisine first introduced in India during the Mughal period (1526-1857 CE).[5] Even today, Burns Road is famous for its roadside eateries offering rich Mughaliana dishes such as *biryani* (rice with meat and different aromatic spices); *haleem* (a stew-like preparation made of wheat, barley, lentils, different spices and meat); *keema-matar* (minced meat with peas); *pasanda* (flattened strips of leg of lamb or goat, marinated and dried in a dish with seasoning); *nihari* (a stew consisting of slow-cooked meat); *paya* (trotters of goat, cow or lamb slow-cooked with various spices); *falooda* (rose syrup mixed with sweet basil seeds and milk); *gulab jamun* (sweetmeat made from milk solids); and *shahi tukra* (rice-bread pudding with dry fruit).

Till the 1980s Burns Road had some of the best eateries that specialised in nihari and paya. The most famous was 'Sabri Nihari' which was said to have camel meat in its nihari. But there were other popular 'nihari spots' here as well, such as the relatively smaller 'Pak Nihari Place'. The smaller nihari eateries mostly catered to those who either couldn't find a table at the more famous eateries or didn't want to stand in line to get into one. Before Pak Nihari Place closed down, sometime in the late 1990s, it used to be a favourite nihari restaurant of mine. I always felt its nihari tasted a lot richer and better than the nihari of its larger competitors. Its owner, a gentleman from Delhi who had migrated to Karachi after Partition, claimed that his cook was one of the few in Karachi with the expertise of preparing nihari like it used to be made during the Mughal era. My friends and I used to visit Pak Nihari Place a lot in the mid-1980s when we were at college. We believed that our robust appetites were best taken care of by the nihari and the soft, crispy *naans* (flatbread) of Pak Nihari Place.

The Mughals were descendants of the second son of the famous thirteenth century Central Asian Mongol warrior and king, Genghis Khan.[6] Genghis Khan's second son was Chagatai Khan whose descendants, through Persian influences and marriages, had converted to Islam. One such descendant was Babur, the ruler of the area which is today part of Uzbekistan in Central Asia. And besides being a descendant of Genghis Khan, also a direct descendant of the fourteenth century Mongol ruler, Tamerlane, marched into India from Afghanistan (after conquering Kabul in 1504 CE). In India, his forces defeated another Muslim ruler, Ibrahim Lodhi. Lodhi was the last king of India's 'Delhi Sultanate'—a sequence of five dynasties of mostly Turkic origin who ruled India between 1206 CE till Babur's invasion in 1526 CE. Lodhi himself, however, was an ethnic Pushtun.

The Mughals were Sunni Muslims[7] who spoke Persian and were highly influenced by Persian culture. As they became more Indianised during their long rule in India, they began to speak a language made up of Persian, Arabic, Turkic and Sanskrit words. This language became known as 'Hindustani'[8] from which evolved Urdu[9] (Urdu is a more Persianised version of Hindustani and mainly emerged during the Mughal era), which today is Pakistan's national language. However, Persian continued to be the language of the Mughal court.

A majority of the Urdu-speaking Muslims who migrated to Pakistan after 1947 claimed to have Mughal ancestry. Indeed while some might actually be of Mughal blood, it is more likely that the direct ancestors of the majority of these migrants were what one of Pakistan's foremost historians, Dr Mubarak Ali, called, 'local Muslims'[10] i.e. Indians (mainly Hindu and Buddhist) who converted to Islam during the lengthy Muslim rule in the region between the thirteenth and nineteenth centuries. According to Dr Ali, most of them converted to Islam to escape Hinduism's caste system and went to the extent of learning Persian so they could find employment in the Mughal administration. But Dr Ali adds that most of them could not and continued to face discrimination because the Persian and Central Asian emigrants who mostly occupied top posts in Mughal administrations considered the local Muslims to be 'second-class Muslims'.[11]

What's more, Dr Ali points out[12] that even during the reign of perhaps the most powerful and popular Mughal king Akbar (1556-1605 CE), when discrimination against Hindus was drastically reduced through some radically inclusive policies, there were still no lower-caste Hindus and local Muslim converts in positions of power. Instead, members of the elite upper-caste Hindu clan, the Rajputs, were employed and worked alongside the Persian and Central Asian Muslim elite in Akbar's administration.

My mother, too, claims Mughal ancestry. An Urdu-speaker (*Mohajir*),[13] she was born in the 1940s in Delhi and migrated with her family to Pakistan in 1947. My father, a Punjabi from the north of the Pakistani Punjab, used to often tease her about her claims, but none would dare say anything adverse about her cooking. She is a terrific cook despite the fact that she had been a working woman (a teacher) throughout her married life, and so could only begin to regularly cook much later in life. Her dinners which she holds for family members and friends on the two Muslim festivals, Eid-ul-Fitar and Eid-ul-Azha, are always popular events. Most of the prepared dishes are of the Mughaliana variety which she had initially learned to cook from her paternal grandmother and then her mother-in-law, my grandmother. But whereas my grandmother would often add a Punjabi flavour to the Mughaliana dishes, my mother, when she did cook in earlier times, would offer a more authentic Mughal cuisine experience.

The cook at the Pak Nihari Place, too, was a Mohajir. He was just seven years old when he came from Delhi with his family to Pakistan in 1950. At the eatery, his employer used to endearingly call him *Wazir-e-Bawarchi-Khana* (Urdu for Minister of the Kitchen). We thought this to be a perfect label for this master nihari-maker. But it was only recently that I realised that his employer had given him this label for a rather more historical reason than I had imagined. This label was not really a tongue-in-cheek moniker to salute the cook's expertise in the kitchen (as we had believed). As it turned out, during Akbar's reign, there was actually a Minister of the Kitchen![14] This minister was given a budget to run an army of cooks and food tasters and look after the affairs of the royal kitchen.

So this is why the eatery's employer used to call his favourite cook, Wazir-e-Bawarchi-Khana. Funny thing is, my friends and I never got to know the cook's name. He was simply known as Wazir. We would go to the eatery so often that the employer would allow us to venture into his cramped kitchen where Wazir would be labouring away with his men to make the most authentic Mughal nihari in Karachi. By then he was in his forties and lived with his wife and three children in a small apartment situated on the floor above the kitchen. The apartment was owned by the employer who had let his cook stay there, free of cost. But Wazir had to pay the electricity, gas and water bills of the apartment himself.

Once, in 1985, a friend of mine and I arrived at the place for lunch from our college which was about twenty-five minutes away by bus. While having our favourite nihari, we were surprisingly joined by Wazir. He was taking a smoke break. Wazir was mostly a reserved person, but on that day he was rather chatty. He told us that he was sick of his job. My friend told him since he was such an expert cook why didn't he open his own eatery. To this Wazir responded (in Urdu): '*Choté Bhai* (younger brother), I don't have the capital. I have a wife and three children to look after. If I leave, the *seth* (Urdu for wealthy employer) will take away the apartment. I don't have the money to rent an apartment, let alone buy one.'

My friend then suggested that he should find employment at an upscale restaurant or a five-star hotel. I remember Wazir just shook his head and snickered, 'Choté Bhai, if I make this kind of nihari there, they will fire me for trying to poison the *babus* and *mems* (Urdu for upper-class men and women). People's tastes are changing. They think the kind of food served here (at Burns Road) is not healthy. All our lives we have eaten this food. My father had nihari every morning since he was a child and by the grace of Allah, he lived to be eighty before he passed away!'

Well, the nihari though heavenly in its taste was certainly not healthy the way Wazir was implying. Nevertheless, we continued to talk and asked how we could help. He was surprised by our question. 'No, no, brothers, this is not why I am talking to you. You are just students and may God give you both long, successful lives. *Mein toh sirf dil ki birhas nikaalney aaya tha aap logon ke paas* (I just wanted to speak to some good people to let off some steam).'

Wazir told us that before his family had migrated to Pakistan in 1950, his father used to own three eateries in Delhi's historic Shahjahanabad area. They had been well-settled and that he sent his two brothers, one sister and him to an 'English-medium school' which had a principal who was a *gori (*white woman, in this case probably British). He said that even when communal riots erupted during the 1947 Partition and one of his father's three eateries was set on fire, the family did not think of migrating and decided to quietly ride out the commotion. However, even three years after the riots (in 1950), Wazir claimed that his father continued to be threatened by men belonging to a militant Hindu group (he didn't tell us the group's name) who wanted him to sell them his eateries at a price which was much lower than their actual worth.

Wazir claimed that his father's ancestors were related to a Mughal governor during the reign of the fourth Mughal king, Jahangir (1605-1627 CE), and when one of his father's brothers was attacked and injured by the militant group, his father panicked and left Delhi with his family to Lahore. With little money and no close relatives in Lahore, the family soon took a bus to Karachi and ended up in a refugee camp.

'My father just ran (from Delhi) with his family and brothers. He gave the keys to his house and eateries to a (Muslim) neighbour and told him he would return after things settled down,' Wazir told us. 'Some of my father's distant relatives who had moved to Pakistan had written to him that there were plenty of empty homes and apartments in Karachi. But when we arrived, these places (which had been vacated by migrating Hindus) had been occupied. We spent eight years languishing in a refugee camp where there was no running water, electricity or food. My father earned a living by becoming a cook at a bureaucrat's house, until he had enough money to rent a small apartment in the Ranchore Line area...'

Wazir and his siblings never went back to school. They all became cooks. Wazir said that when his father managed to travel back to Delhi in 1959 (to reclaim his house and eateries), they had been sold by his neighbour who was nowhere to be found. The father returned to Pakistan and worked at the bungalows of wealthy industrialists and bureaucrats as a cook till he retired in 1981. Wazir lamented his wasted childhood when his family had to squat for years in a refugee camp. He then grew up in a shabby little apartment at Karachi's Ranchore Line area but was delighted to land a job as a cook at a hotel in 1964 (when he was twenty-one). In 1966 he got a better paying job as a 'head waiter' at the Lido Nightclub.

'*Zabardast daur tha, bhai* (It was a great time, brothers)', he had told us, smiling widely. 'I used to get Rs 25 daily (as wages), but lots of tips from the club's drunk clientele,' he laughed. 'But sometimes I used to get drunk myself after drinking from leftover whisky bottles. My mother used to throw a fit and my father refused to talk to me ... that is until I showed him the money which I had made through tips. Rs 100-150 weekly! This was what many people who were better off than us used to make as clerks at the time.'

In 1970, from 'head waiter', Wazir became a cook at the club and then in 1973 a bartender at another club called Oasis. By then he was making Rs 600 a month (salary plus tips). This is when he got married to a neighbour's daughter, a marriage arranged by the couple's parents. The wife, too, was from Delhi and her family had migrated in 1948. 'My wife's family was very strict. Even though she did not have a problem with my work at the club, her parents wanted me to do something else,' Wazir had told us, laughingly. 'Rs 600 a month was pretty decent money to make for a man of my class in those days. I used to take my wife to the cinema every Sunday and she was happy, but her father kept taunting us, saying that my money smelled of wine (*iské paison sé sharaab ki boo aati hai*). He was just jealous. He was a low-ranking official at the Income Tax Department and was making less money than I was. And truth is, I knew he used to take bribes from people, yet he found what I did immoral...'

In 1974, Wazir's first child was born. In 1975, he quit his job and began working at the Pak Nihari Place. Interestingly, according to Wazir, he met the owner of Pak Nihari at Oasis: '*Seth sahib* used to come to the club every Thursday. He was a friend of the businessman in whose bungalow my father used to work. He always told me that my father made excellent nihari and that he would hire him for the nihari eatery he was planning to set up on Burns Road. One day I told him that I could make even better nihari. So the next day he called me over to his house and asked me to make nihari for his family. I did and they all loved it. His wife asked me to work at their bungalow as a cook, but I politely refused. Then seth sahib came the next week to the club and told me he would give me double of what I was making at the club if I would become a cook at his eatery. I still said "no", until he offered to let me stay with my family at the apartment he owned in the building where he was planning to launch his eatery. I immediately agreed. With a wife and a child, my father's apartment was becoming cramped and I wanted to stay away from my father-in-law.'

So Wazir began working at the eatery which was established in late 1975. I first met him here in, I think, 1983. I stopped visiting the place from the early 1990s onwards, mainly due to the vulnerable political situation in Karachi at that time. The state and government had launched an operation against the Mohajir nationalist party, the Muttahida Qaumi Movment (MQM)[15] in 1992. Burns Road being one of the many Mohajir-majority areas of Karachi, it often witnessed terrible violence. I last met Wazir in 1993. He was still working at the eatery and was now over fifty. He had managed to get his children a reasonably decent education from government schools. However, his eldest son, Waqar, had joined the MQM in 1991 and was arrested in 1992 for inciting a riot. Somehow, Wazir managed to convince the seth to bail him out.

In 1991, Wazir had travelled to Delhi in the hope of reclaiming his father's lost property. But he had no clue how to. He told me (in 1993), 'I don't know why I went. I have some relatives there but they didn't even ask me to stay with them. So I stayed in a rest house. But I did manage to locate the neighbour who had sold my father's property. But he was now living in poverty.'

Apparently, the neighbour had invested the money he had made from the sale in a business which had gone south very quickly. 'He was living in a hut with his wife in the Old Delhi area,' Wazir told me. 'His children had abandoned him. It was very sad. The old man told me, "Son, look how we were once kings and princes (Mughals); and now look what has become of us." So I told him to come with me to Pakistan. He said he wouldn't be able to face my father. I told him my father had passed away. Then he asked what I did and I told him I was a cook. He went quiet and after a pause, he repeated, "Son, look what has become of us, we were once sons and daughters of kings..."'

Wazir said this bothered him and he told him off. 'I said, what I do is respectable. We might have been part of some royal nobility once but I make a very noble nihari (shahi nihari) now,' Wazir had sniggered.

I never saw Wazir again. Eleven years later, in 2004, I decided to visit the eatery again to see what had become of him. But when I reached the spot, there was no eatery there. In its place now was a pharmacy. So I asked the owner of the pharmacy what had become of the eatery. 'The owners fought among themselves and then sold it,' he told me.

Owners? But there had been just one owner.

The pharmacy owner clarified, 'Before passing away, that owner sold the restaurant to his cook and the cook's two other brothers at a very low price. But the brothers fought among themselves and sold it to me in 1999. Two of the brothers opened a restaurant in the Clifton area and the one who was the cook (at the eatery) left to live with his son in Nairobi.'

Nairobi?

Indeed. The owner informed me that the cook's eldest son who had been arrested in 1991 had skipped his hearing at the Sindh High Court in 1994 and escaped to Kenya. There he had set up a business and after the business was well-established, he had sent word to his parents to live with him there. He didn't know where the cook's other children were.

And the business that his son had established in Nairobi?

An eatery. Most probably, Mughaliana!

9

A Return to the Womb

After dropping out from Karachi University in early 1990 where I had enrolled as a student of Political Science, I joined *Mag*, which, at the time was Pakistan's largest-circulated English weekly and part of the equally large Jang Group of Newspapers. Many of my early assignments were rather drab until in 1992 when after spending weeks roaming the 'most sensitive' areas of Karachi for a feature on the military's operation against the so-called militants belonging to the Mohajir ethno-nationalist outfit—the Mutahidda Qaumi Movement (MQM)—I managed to break into the major league of investigative journalism. Or so I thought.

The feature which was eventually published across almost ten pages of the magazine attracted a lot of praise from my senior colleagues and readers alike. Even as I was basking in its glory and expecting my editor, an empathetic lady called Samra Niazi, to hand me another prized political assignment, she asked me to cover a conference on Islamic banking. I had no idea what that was nor was I interested. What on earth was Islamic banking, I had asked? I think this was the period when the concept of Islamic banking was just about to rear its head in Pakistan. So my editor asked me to visit the conference and find out what it was all about.

Grumbling and groaning, I reached the venue of the conference where I spent more time (successfully) flirting with a lady reporter of an English daily and then (unsuccessfully) with another one until I decided to sit through at least some of the presentations being made by bankers and economists who incidentally were all men. I found the presentations extremely tedious and I was just not able to gauge the difference between Islamic banking and regular banking. There was hardly any difference between the two, really, at least to my mind. I also remember one of the participants asking a speaker whether the existing banking system in place in Pakistan was un-Islamic. I don't remember what his reply was.

One of the final speakers at the event was a young banker-economist called Yasin Jalal. He looked to be in his mid-twenties. Immaculately dressed in a grey suit, blue shirt and a red tie, Yasin was a tad stocky. He had a longish black beard (but no moustache) and squinty grey eyes. His Urdu was fluent, and so was his English (whenever he chose to speak it); but he spoke it in a heavy British accent. His presentation I found to be as tedious as the ones that had come and gone before his, until he informed the audience that his great-great-grandfather had fought against the British during the violent 1857 'Sepoy Mutiny'. The mutiny, remembered as a 'war of independence' in India and Pakistan, was an uprising against British rule. It was sparked off by Hindu and Muslim soldiers in the British East India Company army complaining about the cartridges they had been issued for their rifles. Hundreds of British and Indian men and women were killed till the commotion was brutally crushed by fresh batches of British soldiers summoned from England.

I can't remember why Yasin mentioned this, but it did get my attention. He didn't say much about it though and so I decided to talk to him after the conference. But I couldn't. Being the sharp, professional young reporter that I had become, I, instead, preferred to investigate the reporter I was (successfully) flirting with at the venue. I asked her to have coffee with me and when she agreed, I forgot all about Mr Yasin's great-great-grandfather. I also failed to file a report on the conference which did not amuse my editor very much. In 1993, I was offered a job as a feature-writer at the Jang Group's vibrant new English daily, *The News International*. One evening, months after I had joined *The News*, when I got out of the elevator to go to my desk, I bumped into the marketing manager of the Jang Group. He was standing in the hallway with a gentleman whom I paid attention to only after the manager casually introduced him to me. It was Yasin Jalal. He was a distant relative of the manager and was there to place an ad for some Islamic banking organisation that he had helped set up in Karachi. After he was done talking with the manager and was headed for the elevator, I briskly walked up to him and introduced myself again. I told him I had been at the conference in which he was a speaker and was very interested in what he was talking about.

I asked him to join me for tea at the cafeteria and explain to me exactly what Islamic banking was. 'For a story?' he asked, in his British accent. 'Maybe,' I replied, 'I just want to explore the possibility of doing one on the subject.' He now looked at me a lot more closely. In those days I had long, unruly hair, a permanent stubble and I always wore a deep blue beret, like the one the legendary South American revolutionary, Che Guevara, used to. On that particular day I was also wearing a flannel shirt (made famous at the time by grunge[1] rockers such as Kurt Cobain and Eddie Vedder) over a pair of completely faded denims that I hadn't washed for, maybe, four months!

So Yasin looked at me for about thirty seconds or so and then smilingly asked, 'Communist?'

'A throwback,' I replied. 'Of an era I was never a part of!'

This made him laugh and he agreed to join me. He didn't smoke but didn't mind if I did. Then off he went trying to make me understand what Islamic banking was. I still came to the conclusion that there was not much difference between what he was saying and what 'normal' banks explained themselves as being. But when he tried again to explain the difference, I changed the topic, 'What was that you were saying about your great-grandfather who fought against the British during the 1857 mutiny?'

'Great-great-grandfather,' he corrected me. Yasin told me his great-great-grandfather (henceforth, g-g-gf) was fourteen when the mutiny erupted. The g-g-gf belonged to a Punjabi family of small traders in Lahore and was studying at an Islamic seminary which had been established during the reign of the last major Mughal Emperor, Aurangzeb (1658-1707). Yasin said when the uprising reached Lahore, his g-g-gf 'defied the wishes of his parents' and joined a group of young Muslims and some Hindus who chose to side with the mutineers. The g-g-gf was captured after he was injured and then thrown into jail. He was eventually sentenced to death by a British military court. The sentence was revoked on the appeal of a respected Sikh officer in the British army. Yasin said that the Sikh's family lived near the g-g-gf's house in Lahore and was on very good terms with his father. Yasin didn't quite explain the contents of the appeal, but just that after his release, the g-g-gf was sent to Delhi by his father to stay with a paternal uncle and aunt. There he was enrolled into a school that, apart from imparting Islamic studies, also taught subjects such as English, mathematics, geography and history.

After graduating from the school, the g-g-gf joined a college ('run by Christian missionaries,' Yasin said). He then bagged a job in the civil services (in Delhi) and married a cousin of his from Lahore. The couple had nine children—four sons and five daughters. The g-g-gf got all his sons educated in 'missionary schools' and then got them enrolled in the Muhammadan Anglo-Oriental (MAO) College (later, Aligarh Muslim University) in Aligarh. The MAO College was founded in 1875 by the famous Muslim scholar and reformist, Sir Syed Ahmad Khan. Khan had emerged as a prominent Muslim voice of reason after the 1857 mutiny had collapsed. Through his writings he appealed to the Muslims of India to acquire modern (British) education and cultivate the sciences, and to avoid the strands of Islam being preached by *mullahs* (clerics) and *pirs* (traditional spiritual leaders). He also asked the Muslims to reform their faith through reason, logic and common sense. He insisted that they shun all kinds of politics and find employment in the British civil services so that a distinct, educated and modern Muslim middle-class could emerge in India (one which could tackle the challenges of British colonialism and Hindu majoritarianism).[2]

Two of the g-g-gf's sons, after graduating from MAO, travelled to England for higher studies. One became a doctor and returned to India, while the other stayed back in England and married an Englishwoman. He was Yasin's great-grandfather. He had four children—three sons and a daughter. They were all educated and raised in England. The sons also married British women. One of them (Yasin's grandfather) had three children, all sons. They, too, were raised and educated in England and (according to Yasin) became British citizens. One of them became Yasin's father when he married a British woman and had four children with her, all born in London. Yasin was one of them, born in 1966. His father owned two restaurants in London. He would often visit Pakistan (which came into existence in 1947) with his British wife and children until the couple divorced in 1975.

Yasin told me his father was greatly distraught by the divorce and 'worried that his children were growing up in an unsuitable environment'. Yasin also said his father, who used to drink a lot and live just like any (white) British middle-class man did, quit drinking and became very religious after the divorce. After coming to an agreement with Yasin's British mother, the father left England and settled in Lahore with his brothers (who had returned from England in the 1970s). The agreement was that the children would visit the father during their summer and winter vacations. But after 1984, they stayed on in Lahore with their father. Yasin didn't tell me why.

Yasin described himself as a 'very religious person' because he believed faith had rescued his father from depression and, in the process, saved his family from completely falling apart. Yasin attended college in Lahore and then travelled to the UK to obtain a degree in Finance. Though he refused to live with his mother, he did (rather proudly) inform me that he had actually tried to convert her to Islam!

'Why?' I had asked.

My questioned surprised him. 'Why not?'

'Didn't she convert when she married your father?' I enquired.

'Only in name,' Yasin said. 'My parents were nominal Muslims. So were my grandparents. They never prayed and, God forgive me, my grandfather had no qualms about enjoying pork ...' he had added, with an embarrassing giggle.

'But they all seemed to be good, educated parents who raised their children well, except for the unfortunate divorce which your parents had to face.' I said.

I was taken aback when he replied: 'The divorce was a blessing.'

'Really?'

'Yes,' said Yasin. 'Had the divorce not taken place, my father would still have been drinking his whisky and his children would have been dining on pork!'

'Your mother used to feed you guys pork?' I asked.

'No, but I'm just saying, we would all have become like our elders,' Yasin replied.

'But you spoke very proudly of your great-great-grandfather at the conference ...' I reminded him.

'I did, but only as a freedom fighter. He changed after that.'

Finally, after (correctly) assuming he had a dual British-Pakistani citizenship, I gathered the courage to ask him that if he was so ashamed of the British-Pakistani part of his heritage, then why he didn't hand back his British citizenship and passport.

'I knew you would ask me this,' he said in his thick British accent.

'And maybe also let go of the British accent?' I added, softly.

'I think we are done here,' he smiled back. 'Thank you for the tea.'

I thanked him as well.

'What are you going to do with this?' he asked.

'With what you have told me?'

'Yes.'

'Whatever you want me to do with it,' I said.

'Fair enough,' he replied. 'It's all yours to do.'

I thanked him again. We shared phone numbers and home addresses. I never got around to writing that story and even though between the late 1990s and 2003, I kept receiving books on Islam from him, I never saw him again. In 2010, I happened to run into the marketing manager of *The News* at a media conference in London. He had just become the marketing director of a large sporting goods company in Qatar. After a bit, it struck me that he was the one who had introduced me to Yasin and so was his relative, albeit a distant one. So I asked him where Yasin was.

'Last I heard he was in London. I think he can't come to Pakistan anymore,' he said.

This surprised me and I asked him why so.

'I believe he was declared to be a member of Hizbut Tarir (HuT),' he said.

HuT is an internationalist pan-Islamic organisation supposedly working to 'reestablish the Islamic caliphate'.[3]

It was formed in 1953 in Jerusalem. Though the organisation is often accused of indulging in the 'politics of hate'[4] and is staunchly anti-West, ironically it is legal in most European countries but banned in Muslim-majority countries such as Pakistan.

He told me that Yasin was accused (he didn't tell me when) by the Pakistan authorities of being an active member of HuT and that he had to quit his job (in a bank in Lahore) and go back to London.

'Was he a member (of HuT)?' I enquired.

'God knows,' he replied. 'He had a pretty good job at a bank in Lahore. But I think he went a little overboard with his preaching.'

'Preaching to whom?' I asked.

'I don't know exactly,' said the manager, 'but I heard he used to hold weekly meetings at his bungalow in Lahore in which some businessmen and his banking colleagues used to discuss how to make everyone as pious as they were,' he smirked.

He then added: 'He had to hastily make a run for London after accusations of him being a HuT member began to circulate. He never came back.'

'Where in London is he staying?' I asked.

'I don't know where,' he replied. And then added, 'But I do know he is staying with his mother.'

10

Their Man from Africa

Lyari is one of Karachi's oldest localities. While today Karachi is Pakistan's largest city, till the early eighteenth century, Karachi had no more than a few fishing villages along its long coastline.[1] In 1729, many of these villages were fortified by the Khan of Kalat[2] and the Talpur rulers of the Sindh province. They named the city Kolachi.[3] The Talpurs were a Sindhi-Baloch dynasty who ruled Sindh between the early eighteenth and mid-nineteenth centuries. A large part of the fortified area became Lyari. At that time, its population was mostly made up of Muslim and Hindu fishermen who spoke Sindhi and Balochi. Karachi was invaded and then conquered by the British in 1839 and it was during the British rule here (1839-1947) that it began to develop into a proper city.

Karachi is also Pakistan's most ethnically diverse city. One of the city's oldest ethnic groups are its dark-skinned men and women, locally known as *Siddhi* or *Shiddhi* and now also referred to sometimes as 'Afro-Pakistanis'.[4] It is believed by some that the word Siddhi/Shiddhi is derived from the Arabic word *Sahibi* which was used for 'respectable' men from North Africa by the ancient Arabs.[5]

A majority of Afro-Pakistanis reside in and around Lyari in Karachi and have been in this area for over 200 years. Some historians have suggested that the first Siddhis to arrive in South Asia came with the army of Arab commander Muhammad-bin-Qasim when he invaded Sindh in 712 CE. They had joined the Arab armies as soldiers when the Arabs first conquered parts of Africa.[6] While Siddhis are also found in areas which today are in India and Sri Lanka, their biggest concentration in the sub-continent is in the main coastal areas of Pakistan, mainly Karachi in Sindh and the Makran in Pakistan's Balochistan province. There are approximately 250,000 Siddhis living in these southern coastal areas of Pakistan today.[7]

It is not known how many Siddhis accompanied Qasim and how many stayed behind, but historians believe that the region's Siddhi population saw a major increase in the sixteenth century when Portuguese traders and explorers began bringing in slaves from Africa, both for labour and to be sold further.[8] Most of these slaves were brought here from Central Africa and belonged to a group of tribes called the Bantu.[9] Those Siddhis who managed to escape slavery settled in various parts of India and a sizeable number travelled to and settled in what today is Karachi and Makran in Pakistan. Here many of them converted to Islam. They became sea-faring fishermen or labourers. In the rest of the Sindh province too they became fishermen in villages along the Indus river, even though some also joined as soldiers in the military of the Talpur dynasty.

The nineteenth century British author and linguist who was also an officer in the British army stationed in Sindh, Sir Richard Burton, wrote in 1851[10] that even at that time, slaves from Africa were still being imported and sold in the coastal areas of Sindh and Makran. Burton also observed that women were more in demand and fetched as much as fifty pounds each. These slaves had been brought in from Madagascar and the East African regions.[11] In Karachi, the Siddhis became fishermen or dockworkers at the city's port which began being developed more rapidly by the British.

Lyari today is regarded as one of South Asia's largest slums. But it appears that it was always a congested locality, even a century-and-a-half ago. When the British conquered Karachi, Burton described the fortified area as teeming with people living in close proximity in mud houses. The area had narrow, unpaved streets and no garbage collection or sewerage system and appalling sanitary conditions. The population was a mix of Hindus and Muslims, mostly Sindhi- and Balochi-speaking and so, there were a sprinkling of mosques, Sufi shrines and Hindu temples in the area.[12] Burton also speaks of 'no less than three brothels' in the area.

The men of Karachi are described by Burton as hard-working but brutish and the women as being fond of colourful clothes and also as 'very loud'. The murder rate was high and alcoholism was rampant. Much of the infrastructural development that the British had initiated after they took over Karachi took place in and around the port area and in places outside the fortified area. Lyari was allowed to fester with no marked changes in its infrastructure and thus suffered the worst of a bubonic plague which spread across the city in 1896. While Karachi recovered and grew rapidly as an important port city in the twentieth century, Lyari has remained its largest working-class locality and slum. Not much has changed here ever since the 1896 plague ravaged it and turned it into a crumbling shantytown.

All this produced a locality riddled with crime, violence and economic desperation. However, this mixture of poverty, overpopulation and crime alongwith the presence of a majority having a proud African lineage has also given birth to a working-class polity, spirituality and aesthetics, all of which have together created a unique cultural scenario. It is this mixture that has created a perception of the Siddhis as being open-minded, large-hearted and hard-working people who are passionate about football, boxing and the movies. Some of the best boxers in Pakistan have emerged from Lyari and the same is the case with football. Lyari is also perhaps the only area in Pakistan where these two sports actually overshadow cricket!

A majority of the Siddhis follow the 'folk Islam' of South Asia,[13] the popular creed of South Asia's Muslims for over 500 years. Not a concrete doctrine, the practice of folk Islam fuses subcontinental folk mores with the ritualism of Sufi Islam and the populist culture of devotional music, charity and festivity found around the shrines of Sufi saints across Pakistan and India. Most Siddhis of Lyari are devotees of the legendary twelfth century Sufi saint, Pir Mangho, whose shrine in the Manghopir area of Karachi is believed to be one of the oldest in the city. The shrine also has hot sulphur springs and a large pond where the shrine's keepers have bred crocodiles for hundreds of years. Feeding these reptiles is considered a divinely ordained ritual.

Siddhis believe the crocodiles are manifestations of the Sufi saint. The shrine is mentioned in ancient texts from the area and also in the writings of nineteenth century British colonialists. Archaeologists have found crocodile bones here which are almost 5,000 years old. They believe that the crocodiles were probably brought here by an ancient flood and have been here ever since. Some historians think that the ritual of feeding these crocodiles was probably first introduced by African slaves who were brought to Sindh from Madagascar. They base this on the fact that for hundreds of years people in Madagascar have believed that crocodiles have supernatural powers.[14]

Every year the Siddhis gather at the 'Siddhi Jat Mela'—an annual festival held on the grounds of the shrine in Manghopir. They come here in hundreds and re-enact the dancing and devotional rituals of their African ancestors. This includes dancing to the beat of drums. Many of these dances have come down to them across the centuries from their ancestors in central and eastern Africa.

For long, Sindh has been an electoral bastion of the left-leaning and populist Pakistan People's Party (PPP). This is surprising since the PPP has always struggled to win seats during elections in Karachi otherwise. Nevertheless, ever since the 1970 election, Lyari has remained a PPP stronghold in Karachi. The area's voters have been returning PPP candidates to the national and Sindh assemblies in every election since 1970. In 1986, when the then chairperson of the PPP, late Benazir Bhutto married Asif Ali Zardari, her wedding reception was held in Lyari and was attended by hundreds of Lyariites.

While crime, poverty and drug and alcohol abuse have long been major problems in Lyari, the situation became almost unmanageable from the early 2000s onward when pitched street battles erupted between the various gangs of the area. Wild and often deadly, Lyari gangsters are more often than not viewed as victims of their circumstances by most Lyari residents. Some have even been projected as Robin Hood-like characters.

The first well-known gangster from the area went by the name of Kala Nag (Black Serpent).[15] He was active in Lyari in the 1960s, peddling hashish and running a network of pickpockets. Kala Nag emerged from poverty to become a local toughie and trained two angry young men from the area, Sheru and Dadal. Both men were huge Hollywood movie fans who loved to drink whisky, smoke hashish and made a living by selling 'tickets in black'[16] outside cinemas. They soon went one up on their mentor and began to encroach upon his business, in the process becoming his rivals. Gang wars became the order of the day, but initially it was largely a battle of fists and knives. Then in 1967, Kala Nag was killed while fleeing from the cops.[17] Sheru and Dadal then turned against each other and battled it out among themselves until the arrival of Kala Nag's son, Allah Baksh, also called 'Kala Nag 2'.[18]

Till the early 1980s, Lyari gangsters were largely involved in the trafficking of hashish, bootlegging and other street crimes. However, the arrival of large quantities of sophisticated weapons and heroin—brought into the city by the large number of Afghan refugees who poured into Pakistan in the wake of the so-called anti-Soviet jihad in Afghanistan—changed that. All the gangs were now arming their henchmen with sophisticated weaponry and had begun to peddle heroin as well. The changing rules of the game and the growing poverty and population in Lyari meant that it was only a matter of time before crimes became even more deadly.

Kala Nag 2 joined hands with one Iqbal Babu and

brushed aside Sheru and Dadal. Nag 2 and Babu's new opponent was Haji Lalu. Lyari was now divided between Babu and Lalu. Both gangs also provided safety to young political radicals on the run from the police during the reactionary General Zia-ul-Haq dictatorship (1977-88). Lalu's gang and the gang operated by Babu and Nag 2 were also constantly battling each other on the streets of Lyari. Extortion had become big business. Babu hired Hanif Bajola, a contract killer, to kill Lalu. Simultaneously, Lalu was training his friend Dadal's orphan son to make a hit on Babu.[19] Soon, Rehman ('Rehman Dakait'), Dadal's teenaged son entered the fray to take revenge for his father's downfall engineered by Babu and Nag 2.

Lalu's son, Arshad Pappu, also arrived on the scene. Yet another generation of Lyari gangsters was now in the making. It would be this generation of gangsters who would eventually turn Lyari into a perpetual battleground which even the police were afraid to enter. The situation was finally brought under some control after 2014, but by then dozens of young men had lost their lives or were in jail.

Rehman, the *chowkidar* (gatekeeper) of the state-run college I was a student of in the early and mid-1980s, was a Siddhi from Lyari. He was in his twenties at that time. His father was a labourer and Rehman, too, had worked as one before bagging a job as chowkidar at the college. And even though I was a leading member of the PPP's student-wing at the college, it was due to Rehman that a couple of friends of mine and I were able to go up on the stage and shake Zardari and Benazir's hands during their wedding in Lyari. Rehman's father, Sadiq, was a loyal foot soldier of the PPP since the 1970s and he was able to get us all up on the beautifully decorated stage on which Benazir had sat on a sofa with Zardari and her mother, Nusrat Bhutto.

The only other time I visited Rehman's modest little home in Lyari was in 1991 when he invited me to his own wedding. I had by then become a journalist. After food was served to the guests, Rehman told me how happy he was to have me at his wedding. He was also keen to have me meet some relatives of his who had come from abroad. I assumed the relatives must have arrived from Muscat in Oman because for decades Siddhis had been hired in that city's police force.[20] But I was surprised when Rehman introduced me to an aged man with a flowing white beard who said he had come from the Republic of Congo (formerly Zaire). What's more, he didn't speak any Urdu but was fluent in the variant of Balochi sprinkled with Swahili words that many Siddhis speak in Pakistan. The old man's mother tongue, however, was Swahili. He could also speak some English and it was in this language that he greeted me, '*Assalam alaikum*, I am big cousin of Sadiq, father of Rehman.'

Rehman almost giggled when the aged man said this because he (Rehman) didn't know any English, other than some slang words he had picked up from Hollywood action films. I waited for the old man to tell me his name but he didn't. So I quickly responded by saying, '*Walaikum assalam*, I am Nadeem, Rehman's friend.' The old man invited me to sit with him and have a cup of tea, even though he didn't drink any himself. 'What is Nadeem?' he asked. At first I couldn't quite understand his question but then realised that he was asking me the meaning of my name. 'Nadeem is a Persian name. It mean's friend,'

I said. 'Irani?' he asked. 'Yes, one can say that. *Farsi* (Persian),' I replied.

Now it was my turn to ask: 'You are from Zaire?'

He nodded his head: 'Yes. Lake area. Big lake area.'

'The Great Lake region,' I said.

'Yes, yes,' he smiled. 'Region of Zaire, Uganda, Kenya and Tanzania. You been to?'

'No, I'm afraid not,' I replied. 'Never been to Africa. How are you related to Rehman?' I asked.

'Big cousin of Sadiq. Sadiq family from Zaire. But he never been to Zaire. I always come to Pakistan to meet,' he explained.

'When did Sadiq's family come to Pakistan?' I asked.

'Sadiq elders come here…' he paused, as if searching for the right word. 'Many year ago,' he finally completed his sentence. Then added: 'Three, four hundred year. Many family here (in Lyari) from Lake area.'

I asked him how come his family was still in Zaire. 'My older people (ancestors) was in white army,' he replied. By this he meant the army of the Belgian colonialists. 'Sadiq older people taken by Western people as *matumwa*.' (Matumwa means 'slave' in Swahili.)

'I tell for many years to Sadiq, come to Zaire, his mother country,' he said. 'But he stay in Pakistan in poor condition,' he lamented.

I asked him whether he was much better off than Sadiq in Zaire.

'Not much, only little much. But Zaire is mother country,' he explained. Another interesting thing he told me was that not all of Sadiq's ancestral relatives in Zaire were Muslim. Some had converted to Christianity and some had retained their tribe's traditional animist beliefs. He said that thirty years ago—that is, twenty years previously from 1991, so most probably in 1971—one such relative of Sadiq's had visited Pakistan and persuaded Sadiq's father (Rehman's grandfather) to travel to Zaire. The grandfather travelled to Zaire with him and worked on a farm there for about a year but came back to Pakistan.

'Zaire not suit him,' the old man said. 'Very hot there, more even than Karachi. Many mosquitoes there, as big as bulls,' he laughed. 'But Sadiq's father visit graves of his older people. They not Muslim but Sadiq father respect them still.' Before leaving, I asked Rehman whether he knew that his ancestors were from Zaire. He told me (in Urdu) that he did: 'We have been hearing stories about them for years. I will tell my children the same stories. But I really don't know where this place (Zaire) really is,' Rehman laughed.

I asked him why he didn't go there to find out, to which he had replied: 'This is our home. My great-great-grandfather, great-grandfather, grandfather, father, mother, siblings and I were all born here. All our elders are buried here. What will I do in Zaire? Our Zaire is right here.'

'A Zaire in Pakistan. Sounds nice,' I smiled.

'Not Pakistan, boss,' Rehman immediately corrected me. 'In Lyari.'

11

A Band's End

About a quarter of the population of Goa, a state in present-day India, is Christian.[1] A majority from this large Christian community in the state are the descendants of Hindus who converted (or were converted) to Christianity by the Portuguese who had set up a permanent settlement in Goa in 1510 CE. These South Asian Christians now also include descendants of 'Luso-Indians' or people of mixed Portuguese and Indian heritage.[2] By the end of the nineteenth century, almost fifty per cent of the population of Goa was Christian (largely Roman Catholic).[3] However, from 1900 onwards, a large number of Goan Christians began to migrate to other cities of India after the state's economy began to decline. It was during this period that many Goan Christians and other Luso-Indians also started to arrive and settle in Karachi because at the time Karachi had begun to expand as an important port city of British India.[4]

When in August 1947, Karachi became part of the newly-born Pakistan, the Goan Christians stayed on in the city. In fact, many Goan Christians living in Karachi had actually supported the founder of Pakistan, Muhammad Ali

Jinnah, when he had campaigned for a separate Muslim-majority country.[5] Till the late 1970s, the Goan Christians of Karachi were involved in the running of well-reputed educational institutions or worked in various white-collar jobs, especially in the service industry. Some of these men and women also married Muslims (often converting to Islam for this purpose). Another profession in which they were heavily involved in was the music scene at the city's popular nightclubs and hotels. Many Christian men and women were regularly hired to sing and play various types of Western music at these places. It was these Goan bands playing in Karachi's many clubs and hotels who first popularised music genres such as jazz and rock 'n' roll among the city's youth. By the late 1960s and early 1970s, there were over twenty well-known rock, pop and jazz bands playing at the various clubs, bars and hotels of Karachi.[6] Almost all of them were made up of young Goan Christian men and women, even though a few young Muslims had begun joining them as well.

In April 1977, the left-leaning and populist government of Zulfikar Ali Bhutto was confronted by a violent protest movement driven by a right-wing alliance of anti-Bhutto parties. Among their demands was the closing down of the nightclubs and a ban on the sale of alcoholic beverages. In a bid to placate the demonstrators, Bhutto agreed and the ban came into effect. The ban on alcohol only applied to the Muslims of Pakistan. Non-Muslim Pakistanis were now required to procure a special permit from the government to buy liquor from 'wine shops' licensed to sell only to non-Muslims.[7] Bhutto was eventually toppled in a reactionary military coup in July 1977 and the military regime which replaced his government turned the ban on clubs and alcohol (which had originally been only a temporary measure taken under pressure) into law in 1979.[8]

While the ban turned the Goan community against Bhutto completely, the irony is that the Goan Christians of Karachi had turned against the Bhutto regime years before it submitted to the demands of the right-wing Opposition. This was mainly due to Bhutto's populist 'socialist policies' which included the nationalisation of various industries and institutions. As part of this policy, the many schools and colleges that were owned and run by the Christians were nationalised as well. When Bhutto agreed to close down the nightclubs in April 1977, it was an even more shattering blow. Many Christian musicians who were earning a livelihood by playing there suddenly lost their jobs. Some continued to earn a living by playing at (the now dry) five-star hotels, but the Christian music scene simply faded away. A number of these out-of-job musicians succumbed to depression and alcoholism. Many completely quit music so much so that when a new local pop music scene emerged from 1988 onwards (at the end of the Zia regime that had been in power since July 1977), this new scene was almost entirely dominated by young Muslims. The Goans seemed to have completely vanished from the music scene.

Many of these young Pakistani Muslims had grown up listening to and learning from the now-aging Christian musicians of yore. While some young Christians too jumped on the new pop bandwagon, their numbers were negligible. Fate had dealt them a strange blow because though most of the new Muslim-dominated acts were competent, they still lacked the fine musicianship of the now-forgotten Goan Christian bands.

I only vaguely remember watching some of these bands perform when, as a child in the 1970s, I used to accompany my parents for dinner at the now defunct Horseshoe Restaurant & Bar on Karachi's Shara-e-Faisal Road and at the 007 restaurant and club situated inside the Beach Luxury Hotel on Queen's Road.

Years later, I got a much better understanding of these musicians when I befriended one Anthony Fernandez at the college that I attended in Karachi, from 1983 till 1987. Saint Patrick's Government College AKA St Pat's had been run by a Goan Christian institution that also ran the St Pat's High School which shared a wall with the college. The college was considered to be one of the finest in the city till it was nationalised in the early 1970s by the Bhutto government. Relatively speaking and compared to the fate of other nationalised colleges, St Pat's had managed to retain at least some of the high standards of teaching and scholarship it was once known for when I enrolled there in late 1983. I befriended Anthony in 1984 mainly because we shared similar music tastes (progressive rock and heavy metal). But unlike me, Anthony was also into various forms of jazz, especially jazz fusion. This was because his father and two older brothers had been musicians in jazz and rock bands.

Anthony's dad had been a drummer in a jazz band which had been formed in the mid-1940s and regularly played at parties thrown by the British residents of Karachi during British rule. Later, the dad formed a brand new band in 1957 (ten years after Pakistan's creation) which played covers of the time's popular rock 'n' roll songs at Hotel Metropole and at the nightclub in Hotel Excelsior. In 1961, he quit the band and joined an advertising firm as an art director. He had four children—three sons and a daughter. Anthony was the youngest, born in 1965. Anthony's two older brothers (both born in the late 1940s) formed a band in 1970 when they were in their early twenties. One brother played the drums and the other, the bass, and they regularly performed rock and pop covers in the ever-expanding numbers of nightclubs, bars, hotels and restaurants in Karachi. According to Anthony, by 1972 one of the brothers had also joined an advertising agency, but continued to play in the band in the evenings. Anthony said both the brothers were making 'some really good money' and were even approached by EMI-Pakistan to record an album of the band's original songs. While this failed to materialise, one of the brothers (the bass player) was invited by a veteran Goan Christian drummer to play in the ensembles formed by composers associated with the then-thriving Pakistani film industry.

For pop songs written and composed for Urdu films, film music directors (all Muslim) and the singers called 'playback vocalists' or 'playback singers' (also all Muslim) were backed up by Goan Christian musicians. Anthony told me that that not only did his brother play on various songs recorded for Urdu films, his band even appeared in a couple of Urdu films in nightclub scenes. The brother received almost twice the amount of money for playing in these ensembles compared to what his band was making. Apparently, the band was making up to Rs 1,500 a week by playing at various clubs, which was quite a decent amount in those days.

In 1975, the bass-playing brother fell in love with a Muslim girl. He had met her when she came over to audition for a singing part in an Urdu film being made in

Karachi. The girl belonged to a Punjabi family. Anthony told me that even though the girl too fell in love with his brother, the brief affair was terminated when the producer of the film (who was from Lahore) decided that it was actually him that the girl was in love with and then proceeded to ask her to marry him, which she promptly did.

I asked Anthony whether he was sure the girl was in love with his brother: 'Yes, yes,' he replied. 'She used to come to our house a lot and my brother used to help her hone her singing talent so she could get the singing part in the film.'

'Then why did she marry the producer?' I asked.

'Because it was him who finally gave her the part!' Anthony replied. The marriage did not last and ended in a divorce 'within months'. Anthony's brother (still in love with her) approached her again, even willing to convert to Islam if she would agree to marry him. She agreed and asked him to approach her father. But when the brother convinced his parents to accompany him, he was told by a friend that the girl had recently tried to commit suicide. Apparently, another producer had promised her a small role in his film, and marriage. According to Anthony, the producer, after having sex with her, refused to recognise her when she turned up on the sets of his film. He had her ejected and on the same day she tried to kill herself by drinking pesticide.

The brother was heartbroken, and began to drink heavily. While he still wanted to marry the girl, he was told by his father 'not to get involved in this messy shit' and stood down. The band played their last gig in March 1977 at the Playboy club before nightclubs were closed down in April 1977. Around the same time, Anthony's sister, Anita, who was an employee at the Karachi office of the now-defunct American airline Pan Am, married a Muslim and became Erum. The eldest brother (the drummer) played in a few other bands after the ban, but the bass-playing brother, who had become an alcoholic, cleaned up, joined an advertising firm (the same one his father was once an employee of) and got married to one Julia in 1980. The couple migrated to the UK in 1983 and never returned to Pakistan.

Anthony said that the oldest brother, however, 'became a bum'. In 1984, Anthony told me, 'He just stays at home, drinking and cursing. He has no friends left.' Egan 'Iggy' Fernandes had been a close friend of his brother, but by 1984, he had passed away too. Egan came from a middle-class Goan Christian family. He was a brilliant guitarist and since he played left-handed, was known as 'Pakistan's Jimi Hendrix'. He began playing for various Goan bands as a teen and would often leave audiences enthralled with his innovative style of playing and his sheer stage presence. Anthony told me that Egan would often visit his brother when the band broke up and after his brother fell into depression. 'He (Egan) was full of energy. He was much younger than my eldest brother, but he kept prompting him to pick up his drumsticks again and play with him.'

Egan became a regular at the Hotel Metropole and continued to play there even after nightclubs were closed down. In 1979, he invited Anthony's brothers to join his group, but they refused. Then in 1980, Egan passed away. He was still in his early twenties. According to Anthony, he had fallen in love with a girl who loved someone else. Fearing rejection, he apparently jumped from the roof of the Hotel Metropole and was immediately killed. Anthony said the news completely devastated his eldest brother. 'Egan was more of a younger brother to him than I was,' Anthony had told me. 'In fact Egan was the one who was keeping my brother from completely losing it.' But it was the same man's death that finally pushed Anthony's brother over the edge. He too passed away (from liver failure) in 1987.

Anthony himself was a pretty good guitar player. He said he was initially taught by Iggy. However, in 1981, his father told him 'to throw the damn thing away and get a proper job'. Things had reached such a pass that in 1984, Anthony told me that Goan families who had encouraged their children to take up music had now begun to abandon it completely. Anthony himself never played in a band, even though he kept his guitar, quietly playing it in his bedroom. There were very few avenues when he came of age.

I first met Anthony's dad in 1993 at the wedding of perhaps one of the finest guitarists produced by Pakistan, Aamir Zaki. Zaki, a genius musician and a troubled soul, was very close to a lot of (former) Goan Christian musicians and invited many of them to his wedding. One of them was a very old man in a three-piece suit—Anthony's dad! Anthony, who was also at the wedding, introduced me to him. I remember for almost an hour the old man talked about his days as a jazz drummer and how Karachi had once been such a great place. Then, suddenly, he went quiet and tears began to roll down his aging cheeks. I didn't know what to do or say. So I put a hand on his shoulder before Anthony came and took him away. He passed away the very next year.

By then Anthony had joined a bank and was doing well there. He got married in 2003, and moved to Canada. Zaki's marriage did not last long. And despite the fact that he rose to become a respected guitarist when he joined the time's leading Pakistani pop band, Vital Signs, his state of mind became increasingly troubled. He passed away in 2017, aged forty-nine. The day I wrote a lengthy obituary on him in *Dawn* newspaper, I received a message in my Facebook inbox from Anthony. He was still in Canada, happily married with two kids. He was still a banker but wrote that after hearing about Zaki's sad demise, he had taken out his guitar and played it for hours.

He then wrote, 'You know, NFP, you should have messaged me before writing that obituary. I could have told you how Zaki, when he was just eight or nine years old, would come to the Hotel Metroplole just to watch Iggy play. Zaki would force his mother to take him there. Iggy would give the young Zaki tips on how to play. And when Iggy passed away, it was as if his soul had entered Zaki's. This was not such a good thing. Because Zaki inherited Iggy's genius but also his troubled soul.'

I wrote to Anthony that since he had taken out his guitar again and was playing it, he should bring it with him the next time he visited Pakistan. Anthony messaged me back: 'NFP, one doesn't need a guitar anymore in Karachi. One needs a gun. And I have none.'

12

Escaping Mao

At my college in Karachi, there were about two dozen Chinese students. They spoke fluent Urdu and lived in the congested Saddar area of Karachi. Two such students (both brothers) became good friends of mine, but, right till our graduation in 1987, I somehow never bothered to enquire about their origins. You see, till about the mid-1980s, colleges and universities in Karachi and Lahore used to have quite a sizeable number of foreign students, mainly from Iran, Egypt, Morocco, Tunisia, Jordan, Nigeria, Yemen, Myanmar, Indonesia, Malaysia, the UAE, Saudi Arabia and from the region which is today called the Palestinian Territories.

Sometimes the Chinese were clubbed together with foreign students, and sometimes they were seen as any other Pakistani. No one really bothered to ask who they were or where they were from. However, a day before we graduated from college, I accompanied one of my Chinese friends to his residence—a three-room apartment in a building behind Saddar's famous Empress Market built by the British in the nineteenth century.

I had lunch at his place (some excellent Chinese food)

and met his parents. The father owned a plumbing business a few metres away from the apartment block. Interestingly, this was the first time I became aware of the fact that my friend was a Christian. Yes, even till the 1980s, one only rarely discussed a person's faith in Pakistan. Anyway, finally, I asked the question. Who were they? The father let out a hearty laugh, 'Well, we are Pakistani!' With an embarrassed smile, I tried to rephrase my inquiry: 'Of course, Uncle ... but what I meant to ask was, that since you speak fluent Chinese and equally fluent Urdu...'

He half-closed his eyes, smiled and sympathetically nodded his head, 'No problem, no problem, young man, I understand.' And then he explained, 'I was born in 1935 in Hubei, a place in China. My father was a cobbler. I was about fourteen when the communist revolution erupted in China (1949). Many Chinese who did not agree with communist ideas migrated with the defeated nationalists to Taiwan. Some, like my family, migrated to the newly-formed country of Pakistan.' A majority of the Chinese families who escaped the revolutionary upheaval in China and migrated to Pakistan came from areas such as Canton, Hopeh, Hakka and Beijing.[1] Most of them were Buddhists but some were Christian and Muslim as well. A bulk of them settled in Karachi's Pakistan Employees Cooperative Housing Society (PECHS), Tariq Road and Saddar areas. Here they continued their family professions, mainly dentistry, acupuncture, shoe-making and the restaurant business. My friend's father, of course, was in plumbing but I have absolutely no idea why and never thought to ask.

Till even today, Chinese restaurants run by the Pakistani-Chinese are some of the most famous in the country's major urban areas, as are Chinese dentists with clinics in Karachi's congested areas such as Saddar, as well as in the city's more 'posh' localities such as Clifton. The Chinese migrants quickly picked up Urdu, and by the 1960s they had blended in, gaining the respect of the locals with their fluency in Urdu, down-to-earth attitude, and solid work ethic. Even though most of the Chinese who settled in Pakistan had escaped the 1949 communist revolution in China, the famous Chinese communist leader Zhou Enlai—during his first visit to Pakistan in 1956—came to eat at a famous (but now defunct) Chinese restaurant in Karachi, the ABC, and had dinner there.[2]

Another batch of Chinese families arrived in Pakistan in the late 1960s. This batch was escaping the social and political turmoil in China whipped up by Mao Zedong's stormy 'Cultural Revolution' (1967-76) in which numerous men and women died. The Chinese who had settled in Karachi soon began holding gatherings in which Chinese children were encouraged to speak in their mother tongue. This was because by the late 1970s, the children of Chinese migrants in Pakistan were largely speaking Urdu and English, and had forgotten their mother tongue.[3]

By the 1980s, the Chinese migrants (who had now become Pakistani citizens) had become so engrained in their adopted country and its culture that they were eating the same blend of Chinese food which they had specially concocted in the 1950s to cater to South Asian tastes. The younger generation had also completely discarded the customary Chinese dress. Marrying within their own community remained a constant, but some younger Chinese men and women began to break with this tradition and started marrying Muslim Pakistanis. It was also during the late 1980s that some Chinese-Pakistanis converted to Islam, but a majority of them remained (and still remain) Christian or Buddhist.

Karachi always had the largest concentration of Pakistani-Chinese. But after the 1980s, many younger Chinese began moving northwards to set up restaurants and dental clinics in Lahore and in Pakistan's capital, Islamabad. Then something unexpected happened. Due to the economic liberalisation in China and the increasingly pragmatic stance of the ruling Communist Party there, many Chinese who had made Pakistan their home began to move back to their ancestral towns and cities in China. Their children who had grown up in Pakistan went for higher studies to universities in Europe and North America and did not return.

With extremist violence erupting in Pakistan, the Pakistani-Chinese community continued to shrink up until the early 2000s. However, due to China's growing economic investment and interest in Pakistan, the community has now begun to regenerate its dwindling numbers.[4] Between 2013 and 2015, at least 15,000 new Chinese men and women[5] (mostly associated with China's growing economic projects in Pakistan) moved to Pakistan. The number is expected to almost double by the end of 2017.[6] My college friend is an example of this revival. His father had passed away in 1989 and was buried in Karachi's largest Christian cemetery, the 'Gora Kabristan' (White Graveyard).[7] My friend flew out to the US in 1991, married an American and became a US citizen. His brother married a Muslim Pakistani girl in 1994, and became a Muslim. The very next year, he accompanied his mother when she visited her ancestral village in China after a gap of almost fifty years and decided to stay in China.

However, in December 2016, I received a sudden visit from a young Chinese lad. His name was Aron Li Stewart. He must have been in his twenties and was an engineer. Li Stewart was also the surname of my Chinese friend at college. And, as it turned out, Aron was his eldest son, born and brought up in the US. Aron told me that in 2013, his father and uncle had planned to exhume the body of their father from the Karachi cemetery and rebury his remains in their ancestral village in China, where their mother was laid to rest. But they never did that because in 2015 they decided to return and resettle in Pakistan.

Aron was expecting a job as an engineer at a large Chinese business project in Islamabad. He told me that the rest of his family would join him in Islamabad soon and so would his uncle and his (the uncle's) wife and children. When bidding goodbye, he smiled and said something in Chinese. I asked him what it meant. He smiled again and explained that the term was an ancient Taoist expression and it meant 'full circle'.

13

The Indus Raga

The Indus is one of the longest rivers in Asia. Even though it originates in the Tibetan Plateau in Central Asia, it becomes wider, stronger, and, if I may, more relevant when it enters the region which today is Pakistan. From Gilgit-Baltistan—one of the northern-most administrative regions of the country—it flows all the way down towards Pakistan's southern-most regions before it falls into the Arabian Sea. The Indus runs across the country's three (out of four main) provinces: The Khyber Pakhtunkhwa (KP); the Punjab; and Sindh. Over the centuries, its banks have spawned a wide variety of cultures, languages and religions.

Five thousand years from the moment the first major civilisation emerged along the Indus,[1] till the creation of Pakistan in 1947, various religions and cultures had come up, thrived and perished there: animist, Hindu, Buddhist, Sikh and Muslim. Islam has become the major faith along the Indus in the last 500 years but the dynamic history of the region has kept even the dominant Muslim cultures along the Indus largely heterogeneous and varied.

Those preaching Islam in the region—especially from the twelfth century onwards—absorbed existing cultural traditions that had evolved for thousands of years along the river, and, in turn, expressed them through the more esoteric strands of Islam (Sufism). Historically, the strand of Sufism which emerged on the banks of Indus (especially in Punjab and all the way across Sindh) consciously eschewed religious orthodoxy, and, at times, even rebelled against it.

My ancestral town, Makhad, is located in the north of the Punjab province. A rugged and hilly area, it is situated on the banks of the roaring river Indus. I have only been to my ancestral home twice. The first time I visited my family home there was in 1980 when I had just entered my teenage years. I remember this visit well because my cousins and I took a ferry that still sails people of Makhad down the river Indus across the Punjab province and all the way to Hyderabad in Sindh, which is just 160 kilometres from Sindh's capital city, Karachi, my place of birth. It is near Karachi that the Indus flows into the Arabian Sea.

The river was red and bulging when we got on the ferry that had just five or six people, including the middle-aged owner of the ferry, Yaqub. As we sailed down past the huge rocks and the desolate little islands of sheer rock protruding from underneath the deep river, the colour of the river began to change. From red it first became muddy brown and then light green when we reached Multan in southern Punjab. The sights and sounds of the scenery also began to change. Once we passed Mianwali, lush green fields and villages replaced hills and rocks. It had taken us a good fifteen hours to reach Multan. Here is where we disembarked, even though the ferry was set to sail all the way to Hyderabad. By then we were just too bushed.

I do wish we had gone further because Yaqub had told us that Alexander the Great had sailed from that point with his army down river Indus, across Sindh, during his exit from India thousands of years ago. Yaqub was from my hometown. He told us that his family had been sailing boats from Makhad to Hyderabad and back for hundreds of years. I remember when we were about 200 kilometres from Multan, Yaqub entertained us by singing a dozen or so folk songs. He said he was neither a singer nor a musician, but like his ancestors, he had picked up various traditional folk songs from settlements on either side of the Indus in Punjab and Sindh. He mostly sang old Punjabi, Saraiki and Sindhi songs, many of them Sufi.

My favourite during the ferry ride was a Sufi *kafi*,[2] *Bullah Ki Jaana Mein Kaun* (Bullah, even to me I am unknown). Penned by the eighteenth century Sufi saint and poet, Bulleh Shah,[3] for over 200 years it has been used as a popular deterrent against the 'orthodox' *ulema* (Islamic preachers/scholars) who have continued to be critical of the strands of Islam that have developed (over centuries) in cultures on both sides of the Indus. Bulleh Shah was born in southern Punjab in 1680 CE[4] and largely preached there in the Punjabi language. He wrote mostly in Punjabi because as opposed to Persian (which was the language of the Indian Mughal court at the time) Punjabi was a 'common man's language'. He also wrote in Saraiki (spoken in south Punjab) and in Sindhi.

The poem is a critical lament against religious orthodoxy. Through his poetry, Shah essentially distances himself from the layers of doctrine that organised religions are wrapped in. Instead, he comes out looking for something free of cultural, political and religious prejudices and perceptions. This is how, he believes, he can discover true humanity and consequently, the Almighty. However, in the end, he realises that by rejecting existing theological, political and social labels, all he is left with is the question: 'Who really am I?' (Bullah Ki Jaana Mein Kaun?)

To him, this feeling of nothingness was close to everything which humans should become (to eschew bigotry and divisions). The nothingness (in the context of traditional Sufi imagery and concepts) is a seamless, almost inexplicable void in which the presence of the Almighty can be felt. It has no room for man-made prejudices. I have tried to translate this eighteenth century Punjabi poem by Shah into English. Rest assured the translation simply fails to capture the power of its original Punjabi—especially when sung by traditional folk singers and *malangs* (Muslim spiritual vagabonds found in and around Sufi shrines in Pakistan and India).

Bulleh, even to me, I am unknown
Not a believer inside the mosque,
Nor a pagan of false rites,
Not the pure amongst the impure,
Neither Moses, nor the Pharaoh...
Bulleya! Even to me, I am not known
Not in the holy Vedas am I,
Nor in opium, neither in wine,
Not in the drunkard's intoxicated craze,
Neither awake, nor in a sleeping daze,
Bulleya! Even to me, I am not known
In happiness, nor in sorrow am I
Neither clean, nor a filthy mire,
Not from water, nor from earth,
Neither fire, nor from air is my birth.
Bulleya! Even to me, I am not known
Not an Arab, nor Punjabi
Neither Hindi, nor Nagauri

Hindu, Turk, nor Peshawari,
Nor do I live in Nadaun
Bulleya! Even to me, I am not known
Differences of faith, I have not known,
From Adam and Eve, I am not born
I am not the name I assume
Not in stillness, nor on the move
Bulleya! Even to me, I am not known
I am the first, I am the last
None other have I ever known
I am the wisest of them all
Bulleh! Do I stand alone?
Bulleya! I am not known.

The other Bulleh Shah poem that Yaqub sang was *Assan Ishaq Namaz Jadoun Neeti Ay* (Ever since I have resolved to say the prayer of love). This one, too, was penned in the eighteenth century, but in the Saraiki language. It is by far Shah's most pointed indictment of the criticism he received from those accusing him of 'distorting faith'. He directly addresses his critics and taunts them for always looking at others and never within their own selves. He also lambasts them for finding spirituality and the Almighty in books, rituals and places of worship, without looking for Him where He really resides i.e. in one's own heart. He dismisses the clergy as being worthless even when compared to a rooster because at least the rooster does his duty of waking people up (instead of stifling them and encouraging them to remain asleep).

You may have read thousands of books,
But have you ever read yourself?
While they all run towards mosques and temples,
They never enter their own hearts.

Your fight against Satan is futile;
Because you have to first fight your own desires.
You seek the one in heaven,
But you never try to reach the one who resides within you.
Ever since I have resolved to say the prayer of love,
I have forgotten the mosque and temple.
The roosters are better than the clerics;
For at least they wake friends who are asleep...
A wine-seller is better than a moneylender,
At least he serves a drink to the thirsty.
Oh, Bulleh, make friends with your critics,
Before they beat you up.
Cleric, leave those books alone,
You just have shallow knowledge.
You need to cleanse yourself from the wines of passion,
Your exterior and interior are both stained.
You continue to enter places of worship,
But when will you enter your own heart?

One song we all sang with Yaqub was *Lal Meri Pat* which has been around for centuries. It was a poem dedicated to the thirteenth century Sufi saint, Lal Shahbaz Qalandar. Lal Shahbaz was born in Afghanistan in 1149 CE.[5] As a young man, he studied religion under various scholars before leaving his home and visiting various countries. He eventually arrived and settled in Sehwan[6]—an ancient city in what is today the province of Sindh in Pakistan.

Shahbaz began preaching a highly esoteric strand of Islam there, and almost immediately attracted devotees from the region's Muslim and Hindu communities. Shahbaz was a rebel and refused to submit to the dictates of the conservative clergy. He mastered various languages, including Sindhi, Pashto, Turkish, Arabic and Sanskrit. He was known for his nonchalant and 'possessed' mannerisms.[7] He died in Sehwan and was buried there. It is also where his shrine stands. Amir Khusro—a poet and scholar from the time of the Delhi Sultanate—after being moved by the stories of Lal Shahbaz, wrote a poem celebrating the life of the saint.[8]

Later, Bulleh Shah and another Sufi saint, Waris Shah (also from Punjab), added some verses to Khusro's poem. By the end of the nineteenth century, roving *fakirs* (spiritual vagabonds) were singing it outside the shrine of Lal Shahbaz. Sung in Punjabi, the poem, though already well-known in Punjab and Sindh, was given a more mainstream make-over in the 1960s by composer, Master Ashiq Hussain. The words of the song were updated by the tragic poet, Saghar Siddiqui,[9] before it was offered to famous Pakistani vocalist and actress, Noor Jahan, to sing. It was this version of the song which became the most popular; and a modern component of Punjab's folk music realm. Later, it was covered by various famous singers of both Pakistan and India.

The song is a whirling tribute to Lal Shahbaz Qalandar. It is often sung with reckless abandon, and to the beat of the entranced South Asian Sufi music genre called the *dhamal*. The song is a particular favourite of the saint's women devotees, who mostly belong to the working class and peasant communities of Punjab and Sindh. They find the words and music to be highly liberating and healing.

Oh Lal, please keep my matters straight;
Long live Lal!
From Sindh and of Sehwan,

Comes the generous Shahbaz Qalandar...
In every step, I trade the path of Qalandar;
Ali[10] *is in my every breath...*
Four of your lamps burn forever,
I've come to burn a fifth one;
Long live Lal!
Oh my mentor, your shrine is high,
Songs are played in sync with the clocks...
Long live Lal!
Ghanan Ghanan (!) is the sound of your drum,
The clocks tick along with it...
Long live Lal...!

The other song that Yaqub sang for us was the haunting *Tarrin Paunda* (it means a kind of plant). It is in the Sindhi language and was first recorded by Allan Fakir (for Radio Pakistan) in the late 1970s. Allan was the quintessential Sindhi folk singer who had mastered the art of expressing the poetry of ancient Sufi saints who had settled along the river Indus in the arid province of Sindh. *Tarrin Paunda* is often mistaken as being the work of eighteenth century Sufi saint Shah Abdul Latif Bhitai. But it was actually authored by Shaikh Ayaz.[11] As a young man, Ayaz was a Marxist and he went on to become a close colleague of the 'father of Sindhi nationalism', G. M. Syed (before they fell out in the 1980s). Ayaz's most prolific period as a writer and poet was between the early 1960s and late 1970s. And it was in the 1970s that he penned *Tarrin Paunda*, which was inspired by the mesmerising poetic style of Sufi saint Shah Abdul Latif Bhitai. The poem is about a man's hope to one day meet his beloved with his natural surroundings in full bloom. The poem was written by Ayaz to be sung in a hypnotic manner, as if the singer was blissfully caught inside an eternal loop of both hope and despair; love and melancholy.

He sings (in Sindhi):

When red roses will bloom, then we will meet;

When those birds will return and make their sounds, then we will meet;

When the tears will trickle down the cheeks like pearls, then we will meet;

Those days of parting were a mistake of youth, so we will meet when there are roses in bloom...'

It was only recently that I found out that Yaqub had passed away in the early 2000s. He must have been in his seventies because he was in his fifties back in 1980. I might never have known about the passing of a man with whom I had shared a long (albeit just one) boat ride. I was told about his passing by one of my cousins who had been with me on that ferry. We had not mentioned Yaqub for over thirty years. It was in 2009 (during my father's funeral) that my cousin suddenly mentioned Yaqub's passing. He did so because the circumstances surrounding his death were extraordinary.

Yaqub had sailed up river Indus towards the KP province so that he could visit a Sufi shrine in one of the towns there. As he was about to enter the place, a huge explosion flattened the place. Dozens of devotees were killed. The explosion was caused by a suicide bomber belonging to an extremist outfit. So, Yaqub, the sailor of the ancient river Indus, the singer of folk songs of spiritual love and peace, befittingly took his last breath at the shrine of one of his beloved Sufi saints—killed there by men full of spite, hatred and a sickness of both the mind and the soul.

14

Drinking Lessons

In April 1977 (as detailed in Chapter 11), the populist government of Zulfikar Ali Bhutto banned the sale of alcohol in Pakistan. It was a temporary order issued after Bhutto had been cornered by a violent protest movement orchestrated by an alliance of right-wing religious parties and other anti-Bhutto outfits. They accused his government of rigging the 1977 election. When Bhutto began talks with the leaders of the alliance, some of their demands included the closure of nightclubs and bars and a prohibition on the sale of alcoholic beverages.[1] The Bhutto regime also cancelled its plans of launching a large casino in Karachi which was to be inaugurated in May 1977. The casino was largely financed by Tufail Shaikh, a Karachi-based businessman who had close links with the Ayub Khan regime (1958-69) and then with the Bhutto government. Sheikh already owned and ran a popular hotel and nightclub in the Saddar area of Karachi and was expecting his new casino to draw in a large number of tourists from the oil-rich Arab countries and Europe. When Bhutto agreed with the opposition to close down the nightclubs and outlaw the sale of alcoholic beverages,

Sheikh was shocked. However, Bhutto told him that it was a temporary measure which he would gradually reverse once things had cooled down.[2]

Bhutto seemed to have convinced himself of this and didn't take his orders very seriously. After all, while nightclubs, bars and liquor stores had closed down, alcoholic beverages were still easily available at hotels and through the back entrances of liquor shops. His non-seriousness about the ban can also be gauged from the manner in which he announced the ban during a press conference. In fact, he didn't say anything about it. Finally, when asked by a reporter, Bhutto smiled and said, 'Yes, alcohol is now banned.' Then lighting up a cigar, he added, 'But cigars are not.'[3]

Hoping to cling on to power for a second five-year-term, Bhutto was eventually toppled in a reactionary military coup a few months later, in July 1977. Two years later, in 1979, the military regime of General Zia-ul-Haq hanged Bhutto for murder through a sham trial. The same year Zia began to roll out laws which he claimed were 'Islamic'. The so-called 'Islamisation' of Pakistan had begun.

Some ministers in Zia's cabinet bemoaned the fact that even though nightclubs and bars had been closed down, alcoholic beverages were still being openly served at social clubs. They said the April 1977 order had loopholes and did not carry any serious punishments against those selling or consuming alcohol. Thus, on 9 February 1979, the Zia regime issued an ordinance called the 'Prohibition (Enforcement of Hudd) Order'.[4] The order proclaimed that selling alcohol to Muslims of Pakistan was illegal and anti-Islamic. Severe punishments and penalties were imposed on Muslims caught selling or drinking alcohol. The order, however, allowed the operation of 'licensed wine shops' which were to be owned and run by members of the non-Muslim communities. These shops were only allowed to sell liquor to non-Muslim Pakistanis and foreigners who now had to get a special permit for this purpose from the government.

Back in the 1980s, I knew a motor mechanic called Naushad. Some of my friends and I used to buy hashish from him. Sometimes we also shared a drink with Naushad in his tiny apartment in Karachi's Golimar area where he lived with his wife and seven children. When tipsy, Naushad would begin talking about how wonderful life was when he was young and unmarried. One day he told us that when riots against the Bhutto regime erupted in March 1977, he came to know about a mob who were planning to attack a liquor store in his area. Even though Naushad, who was in his late twenties at the time, was a supporter of Bhutto's Pakistan People's Party, he could not restrain himself from joining the mob so that he could loot as much booze as possible from the store. 'I managed to bring home at least twelve bottles of beer and whisky' he told us (in Urdu), laughing. So a friend of mine asked him, 'What happened when you finished drinking the looted bottles and then alcohol was banned?' Naushad suddenly became morose and just shrugged his shoulders: 'We were young. Uneducated people like me can't see beyond our nose. All the mobs who were attacking the liquor shops were looting it. We never thought Bhutto Sahib would ban alcohol.' Naushad then began to moan and groan about how expensive it had become to get even a small bottle of whisky from the licensed wine shops.

The largest number of such wine shops were in

Pakistan's Sindh and Balochistan provinces, especially in their capital cities, Karachi and Quetta. Their number doubled during the military dictatorship of General Pervez Musharraf (1999-2008) and then during the coalition government of Pakistan's three leading 'liberal' parties—the Pakistan People's Party, the Awami National Party and the Muttahida Qaumi Movement—between 2008 and 2013. Musharraf had come to power in 1999 through a coup and viewed himself as an 'enlightened moderate'.[5] He tried to do away with the 1979 Ordinance but could not due to the electoral compulsions of his own party, the Pakistan Muslim League (Quaid). However, acquiring alcoholic beverages from licensed liquor stores became much easier for Muslims during the Musharraf regime. But then over ninety per cent of consumers of these stores had always been Muslim.[6]

Religious groups and parties have continued to lament that Pakistani governments have been too lenient in imposing the 1979 Ordinance whereas those opposed to the Ordinance have maintained that prohibition has resulted in the emergence of bootlegging mafias and the proliferation of tainted alcohol ('moonshine') which has caused the deaths of hundreds of Pakistanis who can't afford the more expensive brands available (for non-Muslims) at the wine shops. They also point out that prohibition had also driven many young Pakistanis to become heroin addicts and that religious outfits hardly ever mention heroin which was far more dangerous than alcohol.

They might have a point. There were just two reported cases of heroin addiction in Pakistan in 1979. But by 1985, Pakistan had the world's second largest population of heroin addicts.[7] The religious lobby has often implied that selling and consuming alcoholic beverages was against the dictates of Islam's holiest book, the Qu'ran. Those who disagree with these lobbies suggest that the Qu'ran does not mention any punishment for drinking liquor [8] but only asks Muslims to avoid having it in excess and to 'leave it aside in order to succeed'.[9] Such debates have increasingly lessened in intensity in Pakistan and acquiring liquor has certainly become a lot easier than it was in the 1980s. In late 2016, a group of petitioners in Karachi moved the Sindh High Court (SHC) against the continuing growth of 'licensed wine shops' in the city. The court ruled in favour of the petitioners and ordered Sindh's provincial government to immediately close down all liquor stores in the province because they were not operating according to the dictates of the 1979 Prohibition Order.[10] The court pointed out that these stores were openly selling liquor to Muslims.

An organisation of wine shop owners in Karachi hired one of Pakistan's leading lawyers and judicial activists, Asma Jahangir, to submit an appeal in the Supreme Court against the SHC's ruling. Jahangir told the court that thousands of people belonging to Pakistan's non-Muslim communities were employed at the shops and would lose their livelihood. She said that the shops were working exactly according to the 1979 Ordinance and that it wasn't their fault that a majority of their customers were Muslim. The Supreme Court struck down the SHC ruling and ordered the re-opening of the shops.[11]

The irony is that the rate of alcoholism witnessed a two-fold growth during the prohibition.[12] Those studying this phenomenon say that alcoholism as a disorder becomes a complex matter to treat in a society where there is a prohibition in place.[13] They say that whereas it is easier for alcoholics from the upper and the middle-classes to get treatment at detoxification centres, it is tough for people with this disorder from the working classes who believe that they can be arrested for confessing that they drank alcohol regularly.[14]

Ever since the late 1970s, anti-alcohol crusaders have maintained that drinking alcohol (by Muslims in Pakistan) was a 'colonial legacy'. They suggest that the habit of drinking alcoholic beverages was imposed on the Muslims of the region by European colonialists. This is how they respond especially when told that all the leading founders of Pakistan, including the highly respected lawyer and politician, Mohammad Ali Jinnah, liked to drink. The truth is that drinking alcoholic beverages is not a 'colonial legacy'. The people of South Asia have been drinking alcohol for over 5,000 years. Interestingly, it is lighter stimulants such as coffee, cigarettes/tobacco and tea which were first introduced in India by the colonialists and all of them are legal in Pakistan.

Recently, the soft drink brand Coca-Cola tried to convince Pakistanis that they should replace tea consumption with their cola. Many Pakistanis responded on social media by suggesting that this was impossible because drinking tea was an integral part of South Asian culture. Drinking tea (or coffee) is a part of various cultures across the world because it is an intoxicant, albeit a mild one. It can only be replaced by another intoxicant. But understandably in a largely dry country such as Pakistan, this aspect of the argument never comes up. South Asians as a whole are usually ambiguous about the use of intoxicants in their respective regions. They have often sought refuge in the explanation that intoxicants were thrust upon them by foreigners.

Yet, 5,000 years ago, the inhabitants of the Indus Valley Civilisation were preparing alcoholic drinks made with sweet and starchy ingredients. In Pakistan's Taxila Museum lies one of the oldest known distillers in the world (dating back to 3500 BCE). It was discovered in the ruins of Mohenjo-daro, and archaeologists believe that it was used to distil oil and alcoholic beverages.

At the time of the emergence of Hinduism's earliest sacred text Rigveda in 1400 BCE, Hindus were drinking alcoholic beverages so much that the Rigveda asked them to desist from the habit.[15] As an alternative, the Rigveda advised them to imbibe a much 'holier' drink, the *Soma*.[16] Soma was made from the extract/juice of an unknown plant which was then fermented. The usage of cannabis too was common during the time of the Rigveda.[17] Cannabis at the time was either eaten or mixed with water or milk as a drink (*bhang*). Unlike alcohol, this intoxicant was not frowned upon by priests.[18] Another drug which is reported to have been common in ancient India was opium. By 1000 BCE opium was being consumed as a medicine by a large number of ancient Indians.[19] By 500 BCE, Soma, *Sura* (beer made from barley) and *Madhu* (honey wine) were also commonly available in India.[20] Some of the earliest Greek sources written after Alexander's invasion of the region (in 325 BCE) mention that after Alexander's army found large vineyards in the hills (most probably in present-day Swat in Pakistan) they believed that Dionysius, the Greek god of wine, had already come to India before Alexander.[21]

The same sources also say that Buddhism outrightly

forbade its adherents from drinking alcohol, stating that Gautama Buddha (483 BCE-400 BCE) had once remarked, 'Drinking ends in madness.'[22] When Xuanzang (Hieun Tsang), the seventh century traveller from China, visited India during the reign of Harsha (who ruled over a large part of north India including present-day Peshawar in Pakistan), he noted that people drank 'wines made from flowers' and some 'strong distilled liquors'.[23]

By the emergence of Muslim rule in India in the thirteenth century CE, alcoholic beverages, bhang and opium were widely available in the region. One of India's foremost historians, the late Abraham Eraly, in his books on the Delhi Sultanate (1206-1526 CE) and Mughal rule (1526-1857 CE) has commented in some detail on the many indulgences of the people of the region under Muslim rule. Eraly informs us that most rulers of the Delhi Sultanate drank wine which was largely produced in India, but some of it was also imported from Afghanistan and Central Asia.[24]

Having opium and bhang was common among the masses. The court's ulema often advised the Sultans to ban intoxicants (especially wine and spirits) but only Sultan Alauddin Khilji (1296-1316) actually imposed a ban on alcoholic beverages.[25] However, illegal distilleries operating outside the cities continued to supply wines and spirits to the populace—including Alauddin's own court officials.[26] Babur, the founder of the mighty Mughal Empire, was an opium-eater[27] and loved to drink fine wines. Though he is reported to have quit drinking during the later years of his life, he did not impose any ban on intoxicants. Ironically, it was the most 'liberal' Mughal king Akbar (1556-1605 CE) who issued the Empire's first major decree against the sale and consumption of alcoholic beverages. The sale and usage of opium and cannabis on the other hand remained legal.[28] But Akbar soon repealed the proclamation and made the indigenous Indian wine 'toddy' (made from coconut palms) entirely legal.[29] Eraly extensively quotes two seventeenth century Western travellers—the Italian Niccolao Mannuci and Edward Terry—who wrote lengthily on Mughal India. Both noted that although the consumption of alcoholic beverages was frequent among court nobles and both Hindu and Muslim commoners, Indians did not drink as much as the Europeans, 'mainly due to the hot weather in India'.[30]

It was only in the late 1600s that sources mention the consumption of tea and coffee in India. The earliest reference to tea in India was made by a German traveller, J. A. Mandelslo, in 1638 CE. He writes that Indians (both Muslim and Hindu) 'use tea as a drug to cleanse the stomach'. Tea was not grown in the region till the mid-nineteenth century[31] and whatever tea there was in India before this came from China.

Coffee, too, was imported (mostly from Arabia) and was a luxury beverage in the Mughal court.[32] But it never caught on in the region as much as tea did. Sources also mention another mild intoxicant, the *paan* (betel leaf). According to the seventeenth century British traveller Thomas Roe, Indians of all faiths and classes 'loved to chew the betel leaf which makes one feel giddy and spittle red'.[33]

Tobacco was unknown in India till the late sixteenth century.[34] It was introduced by the Portuguese during Akbar's reign.[35] Akbar tried it in a hookah (which, too, was an innovation imported from Arabia). Some of his advisers asked him to ban it but Akbar enjoyed it and allowed its sale.[36] Tobacco soon caught on, becoming widespread, especially when cigarettes were introduced in the region in the early 1900s. The last major Mughal king Aurangzeb (1658-1707 CE) banned liquor but illegal distilleries continued to churn out spirits.[37] The British colonialists banned opium, but regulated and taxed alcoholic beverages, hashish, tea and tobacco[38] throughout the late nineteenth and early twentieth centuries. Some of these revenue-generating methods were adopted by India and Pakistan when the British left in 1947.

However, as already mentioned, in 1977, Pakistan banned the sale of liquor to Muslims. In their 2008 research on alcohol consumption in Pakistan, Waseem Haider and M. Aslam Chaudhry discovered that despite the 1977 prohibition on alcohol and the further strengthening of this prohibition in 1979, alcohol consumption remained prevalent (mainly due to bootlegging and illegal distilleries). As proven by the region's history, it is almost impossible to legislate morality.[39]

We stopped meeting Naushad when we gave up smoking hashish some time in the early 1990s. A friend once told me (in the late 1990s) that Naushad had been arrested and was in jail for selling heroin. I never saw him again. But while doing this chapter, another exchange between Naushad and a friend of mine came to mind. Golimar, the congested area where Naushad lived, had numerous drug dens, some in plain sight. So a few days after Naushad had told us how he had joined a mob to loot liquor stores in 1977, my friend asked him why didn't he gather a mob and loot the drug dens in his area. I remember Naushad in his typical manner had just shrugged his shoulders and said: 'Because nobody has asked me to.'

15

Wearing the Inside Out

In 2014, my brother-in-law, an industrialist, told me that when he saw a labourer at one of his textile factories struggling to complete a task which he was given by the foreman, he (my brother-in-law) noticed that it was due to what the worker was wearing that he was unable to convincingly complete the chore. I don't quite remember what the task was, but I do remember my brother-in-law telling me that he advised the foreman to ask the worker to wear the overalls that were provided to almost all workers of the factory. The foreman did just that but only to be told by the worker that wearing anything other than kameez-shalwar was 'un-Islamic'. My brother-in-law then directly approached the worker and asked him exactly what was so Islamic about the kameez-shalwar. The worker simply replied, 'I don't know. The *moulvi sahib* (preacher) of the mosque where I go to say my daily prayers said this.'

The kameez-shalwar is a traditional outfit commonly worn in both parts of India and Pakistan, by both men and women. Sometime in 1972, it was declared as Pakistan's national dress.[1] Till then it was largely considered a working-class dress. It was also associated with the Pushtun, Sindhi and Baloch ethnic communities in the country's rural areas. Before kameez-shalwar became the national dress, most urban middle and upper-class Pakistanis wore Western clothes (mainly trousers, shirt, and, if need be, suit/jacket). Men sometimes wore the *sherwani (*long coat-like garment*)* with *tang pajama* (tight trousers) and women, the *kameez* with *churidar pajama* (tight trousers)—clothing that dated back to the time of Muslim rule (thirteenth to nineteenth centuries) in India. Mostly well-to-do Muslim and Hindu men and women wore these clothes. Women also wore the saree—a dress which is said to have originated thousands of years ago during the period of the Indus Valley Civilisation.[2] The saree is still popular in India, but has almost vanished from Pakistan.

The kameez-shalwar became widely popular when the chairman of the populist and left-leaning Pakistan People's Party, Z. A. Bhutto, began to wear it during his public rallies. He started to pair it with a 'Mao cap' after he became President of Pakistan (in 1971) and then Prime Minister (in 1973). In 1973, it was declared as *awami libas* (people's dress) and then as the national dress. No law was passed regarding the kameez-shalwar. However, it began to be drummed up as a national dress in textbooks and the state media and automatically came to be considered so. So from being the dress of the working-classes and the rural people, Bhutto had turned the kameez-shalwar into a populist political statement. But from the early 1980s onwards, it began to be increasingly associated with Islam. This happened when the reactionary military dictatorship of General Zia-ul-Haq (1977-1988) made it compulsory for government and state officials to start wearing it to work.[3] The move was explained as part of Zia's 'Islamisation' process, but never explained just how this was in anyway related to Islam. Some believe that the perception that the kameez-shalwar was an Islamic dress largely began to be formed when those Pakistanis who often wore Western-style clothes began to wear the kameez-shalwar in mosques during Friday prayers. The Zia regime also discouraged women from wearing the saree[4] and more and more women began to adopt the kameez-shalwar. The state-owned media also began to label the saree as a 'Hindu dress'.[5] In 1982, the regime went to the extent of asking the state-owned TV channel, PTV, to always show good characters (in TV plays) wearing kameez-shalwar. 'Bad characters' were typically shown as wearing Western clothes.[6]

The kameez-shalwar actually predates Islam by hundreds of years. It probably originated during the largely Buddhist Kushan rule in the second century CE.[7] It was a syncretic empire that had its origins in Central Asia and included large parts of what today is northern Pakistan. A dress with loose baggy trousers and a kameez-like shirt was introduced by the dynasty in this region. It was adopted by the Pushtun tribes of areas which today live in present-day Pakistan. Various versions of this dress evolved and spread all over the Indian subcontinent. Today, most Pakistanis wear kameez-shalwar as an expression of national identity or simply because they grew up wearing it. But there are still some sections of the society which regard it as an 'Islamic dress'. And these are the same sections who over the years have modified it to accommodate elements they have adopted from items of Arab clothing, such as the *hijab* (veil), the *thawb* (robe), etc. These they brought back from their stay (as expats) in the oil-rich but conservative Arab countries, mostly in the last twenty-five years or so.

In the summer of 2014, I was at a marketing and media conference in Dubai, organised by a British cultural organisation. Delegates had been invited from various Asian and African countries whereas the speakers were largely from Britain. The conference also offered many media workshops. At one such workshop conducted by the marketing head of a British organisation, I sat beside a young Indonesian man. Every time the British marketing head exhibited slides with images of employees working at the offices of the organisation in the UK, the Indonesian would shake his head and frown. Finally, after about five such slides, the Indonesian raised his hand.

'Excuse me,' he said. The Briton stopped his presentation: 'Yes?'

The Indonesian stood up and started to speak: 'Why do you people have to continuously show Muslim women in hijabs in your pictures?' The Briton seemed surprised by the question. Raising an eyebrow, he said: 'I am sorry but I don't understand. What do you mean?' As he said this, he quickly but closely studied the Indonesian. He had a longish beard and was wearing a white skull cap and kurta-pajama. The Indonesian spoke again: 'Every time you people speak about diversity in your country, you show Muslim women in hijabs. Why is that?' he asked.

The Briton looking perplexed, said: 'Sorry, but I still don't understand your question.' Another hand went up. It was of a young Egyptian man with a trendy goatee. He was wearing blue jeans and a T-shirt. 'May I?' he asked.

'Yes, please,' the Briton replied, as if relieved by the intervention. The Egyptian lad stood up and said, 'Is this the only way for you guys to show Muslim women?' he asked.

'How else do you want us to show them?' the Briton replied, this time with a hint of annoyance in his voice. Before the Egyptian could answer, the Indonesian man, who was still standing, interrupted, 'No, no, this was not what I meant!'

A young Pakistani woman (in a hijab) who was seated in front of us, nodded rather vigorously. 'Yes, yes, he did not mean that,' she quietly said, as if to herself. The Egyptian, while placing himself back on his seat, smiled: 'I know, brother, this was not what you meant. But this is what I mean.'

The Briton suddenly raised his voice, 'Gentlemen, we are getting distracted here. This has nothing to do with the subject of the workshop. Can we continue with what we are here for?' And we did. But I was fascinated by this short, sharp exchange. So during the coffee break I quickly approached the Indonesian man. After introducing myself, I asked him what was it that he was trying to point out in his question. He said, 'These people (the Westerners) refuse to understand the meaning of our faith. They think it's only about how we look.'

I slowly nodded my head and then politely added: 'I think it cuts both ways. How well do we understand their faith?' The Indonesian was quick with his reply: 'What faith?'

'Well, for example, Christianity,' I retorted. 'Or the fact that some might have no faith at all. That too is a faith, no?' The Indonesian smiled: 'My question to him was more about their need to understand our faith a little more deeply.' I again nodded my head, 'Well, yes, it is a rather stereotypical way to show Muslims in beards and hijabs.' Hearing this the Indonesian almost spilled his coffee: 'No, no, friend, not stereotypical. That is the correct way of showing us Muslims. But they (the Westerners) need to look deeper still.' I couldn't help but ask (very politely): 'So, this means, showing a Muslim with no beard or hijab is not correct. But showing Muslims in beards or hijab is, but needs to be looked at in a deeper manner?'

'Yes!' came the answer. 'That is what I meant. You get it because you are Muslim.'

'Actually, I don't,' I shot back, again very politely. Then added, 'Maybe I should look deeper still?' He went quiet for a bit, then striking a thoughtful pose, he nodded and softly proclaimed, 'Indeed, indeed...' Saying this, he took his cup of coffee and left. Just like that. Later that day, I bumped into the Egyptian guy in the smoking area. He said that he agreed with the Indonesian man's question, but not with his intent. Hearing this I shared with him my exchange with the Indonesian. He laughed, 'You see, Westerners love to dress people up with identities. This makes them feel superior. And we (the Muslims) love to dress up for them.'

This was interesting. He continued, 'Who gave us this look (of hijab and beard)? We now dress up exactly the way the West perceives us. We love to get their attention. Muslims like you and I will never be in those pictures, bro,' he laughed again. The next evening the Egyptian, an Algerian, a Chinese, another Pakistani and I strolled into a restaurant at the hotel we were all staying in. The Briton was already there. Though much of our conversation with him was about the workshop, the Egyptian did bring up the hijab question again.

'Listen,' said the Briton, 'when we have to exhibit diversity in a poster or a picture, we often show some Caucasians, some blacks, some Chinese and so on. So, when we have to exhibit religious diversity, we show people of different faiths together. Now tell me, how are we to tell that a man or a woman is Muslim? That's why the hijab and all.'

'Makes sense,' said the Egyptian. 'Good, now let's drink up, already!' said the Briton, raising his glass. But just as we were about to, the Egyptian interrupted: 'But ... if, in a picture, a Muslim woman has to be shown in a hijab and a Muslim man in a beard to portray that they were Muslim, I was wondering how would you guys show a Christian? Do you dress him up like the Pope? How would we know he was Christian?'

Everyone at the table sniggered, with the Chinese guy saying that at least the Chinese are not shown wearing a Mao cap anymore to show that they were from China. The Briton cracked a resigned smile, 'Okay, Mr Cairo, you made your point.' Mr Cairo raised his glass, 'Oh, I was just wondering, that's all. Cheers.'

16

It Came from the West

When my mother was in her teens, in the 1950s, she was coaxed by her cousins and friends to accompany them to watch a 1956 Hollywood film, *Rock Around The Clock*. By the time the film was over, young men and women had already destroyed the seats of the cinema where it was showing. My mother told me that the cinema had to stop playing the film because, according to her, it had continued to 'cause riots'. When I asked her why, she said, 'It wasn't anything serious; it wasn't that the teens were fighting; they used to just stand on their seats to dance, whistle, hoot, shout, not realising they were wrecking the place.' Yes, but why, I had asked her again. 'Because of the music, I suppose,' she had answered. 'None of us had ever heard music like that. We had no clue what it was; but it just made us go crazy!'

The music my mother was talking about was rock 'n' roll. Born in the United States in the early 1950s, rock 'n' roll took elements from other American music genres such as jazz, bluegrass, country-western and the blues, and sped up this mixture to create what began to be called rock 'n' roll. But just as my mother had told me, till the mid-1950s, a majority of Pakistanis had never heard anything like it—until, of course, the release of *Rock Around The Clock* in the cinemas of Karachi and Lahore. Yet, even when such Western music genres began to reach Pakistan, mainly from the late 1950s onwards, they were adopted almost entirely by the country's Goan Christian communities.[1] Very few Muslims were ever part of the bands who were playing jazz and rock 'n' roll at hotels and nightclubs, even though they (the Muslims) were some of these bands' most prominent patrons and fans.

In 1966, the famous Pakistani film actor and teenage heartthrob, Waheed Murad, produced and acted in an Urdu film, *Armaan* (Desire) which featured the song, *Koko Korena*. Sung by the young playback singer, Ahmad Rushdi, it became perhaps the first Urdu song that was heavily influenced by western music genres. The song became a smash hit among the country's urban youth. 'Pop' songs then became a norm in Urdu films after this, especially in the 1970s. Pop music in Pakistan in the 1970s was almost entirely associated with and tied to the country's film industry that was peaking in that decade (before collapsing and withering away from the 1980s onwards). Tastes in fashion, lifestyle and music among the general public were largely informed by Pakistani films of the era. Through films, actors, directors and musicians paraded new fashions and sounds arriving from the West and fused them with the social and creative dynamics of traditional Pakistani art forms and in the process developed a creative and effusive syntheses uniquely Pakistani in essence. A majority of the period's musicians were all associated with the film industry as playback singers, composers, instrumentalists, etc. Here was where all the fame (and fortune) was.

There was nothing called Pakistani pop, though. But since composers scoring songs for Pakistani films had increasingly begun to sprinkle their songs with influences, references and sonic allusions from Western pop music, certain young playback singers came to be seen as specialists in this style. So every time a composer would score a song (for a film) that bore heavy Western pop influences, he would usually invite a Ahmad Rushdi or a Runa Laila to sing it. Rushdi had been singing jaunty songs for Pakistani films since the 1960s, but in the 1970s, he became a pop specialist. Runa Laila, a young trendy vocalist, was Rushdi's female contemporary. Their voices became *de rigueur* in songs composed for films that were made to attract young urban middle-class Pakistanis.

Rushdi and Laila's popularity in these kind of films prompted a film producer to pick up a guitar-wielding hippie drifter from Karachi's Hill Park and ask him to try his luck singing songs for films targeted at young audiences. Before he was hired to sing his first song for films (in 1974), Alamgir was a twenty-one-year-old hippie, who could often be seen singing songs and playing his old acoustic guitar at Karachi's Hill Park.[2] Sometimes he would do it for a cup of tea, sometimes for a cigarette and sometimes for food (when he remembered that he had to eat too to survive). Soon, Runa, Rushdi and Alamgir became pop specialists in the film industry. Pakistani film songs influenced by Western pop music peaked in the mid-1970s, so much so that two of the period's most prolific playback singers, Mehdi Hassan and Nayara Noor, too, (for a while) agreed to venture into this new domain with surprisingly successful results.

As this genre of Pakistani pop (later labelled as 'filmi-pop'[3]) began to expand, composer Robin Ghosh became its leading exponent when he began to use sonic elements of the time's famous Western pop acts, such as the Bee Gees and The Carpenters, in his songs.

But, interestingly, to make the songs sound distinctively Pakistani, he used conventional playback singers like Mehdi Hassan and Nayara Noor. The only overtly pop singer that he used for his compositions was Alamgir. This resulted in the decline of Rushdi and Laila. At the same time, Alamgir began to write and compose his own songs. In 1977, he was given the task to collaborate with composer Karim Shuhabuddin to score the songs for the Urdu film *Bobby & Julie* (1977). The film was a flop, but its soundtrack was a commercial success. One of the songs in the film, *Dekha Na Tha*, turned Alamgir into the country's first bona fide pop star when he performed it on TV (PTV) along with a visiting female Turkish pop singer, Naazi. *Dekha Na Tha* incorporated elements from the disco sounds of that time and also made sonic allusions to 1970's 'Glam-Rock' style.

Alamgir's success in this regard inspired a number of young singers to bypass the film industry and write, record and release their own songs. Another singer, Mohammed Ali Sheikhi, recorded an album of his own Urdu pop songs without banking on the film industry's influence and muscle. Sheikhi, who eventually did go on to sing a few songs for films, was soon followed by pop vocalists such as Khalid Waheed and Tehseen Javed. But another reason why men such as Alamgir and Sheikhi were breaking away from films was the fact that after the July 1977 reactionary military coup of General Zia-ul-Haq, the Pakistani film industry began its steady commercial and creative decline.

It would almost completely collapse after 1979, burdened by the weight of stricter censor policies, the retreat of the industry's main paying audiences (the urban middle-class), the arrival of the VCR, and the creeping creative corrosion within the industry itself. Many playback singers failed to survive the collapse, and pop singers such as Alamgir and Sheikhi had to now bank on TV and album sales to survive.

Disco music had taken the US and Europe by storm in the mid-1970s, but it didn't become popular in Pakistan till about 1979, especially when disco acts such as Boney M, Donna Summer and Eruption began to concentrate on releasing their albums in the Asian and Middle Eastern markets. This was mainly due to the fact that just when, from 1979 onward, disco's market had begun to recede in the US and Europe, it began to expand in many Asian and Middle Eastern countries. In Pakistan, for example, between 1979 and 1983, disco music was being bought, heard and admired by people across classes. Indeed, pop songs from Urdu films, too, had mass appeal, but they were simply tinged with Western pop influences and were being dished out by Pakistanis. But thanks to disco, never had such a cross section of society become fans of Western music acts. Besides Boney M and Eruption, other popular acts were ABBA and Michael Jackson. I remember back in 1983 when I used to take a public bus from near my house to go to my college in Karachi, these buses would often play Eruption's *One Way Ticket*, Boney M's *Daddy Cool* and all of Michael Jackson's *Thriller* album.

It is interesting to note that disco became big in Pakistan during a reactionary military dictatorship that actually began to Islamise Pakistan like never before. Around this time, a brother-sister duo—Nazia and Zoheb—decided to tap into the growing disco trend in Pakistan. Hailing from Karachi, the duo exploded onto the scene with the country's first ever Urdu disco album, *Disco Deewane* (1980). Recorded in London under the supervision of famous British-Indian disco producer, Biddu, the album was studded with classic disco beats and dynamics fused with Pakistani 'filmi' sensibilities and lyricism. Released in Pakistan by EMI-Pakistan, within days it became the music label's biggest-selling album. Young Pakistanis constantly called Radio Pakistan asking it to play songs from the album and even the somber PTV ran a crude video or two. But when a 'religious advisor' of the Zia regime (in Lahore) saw the video of the album's title song on PTV, he complained to Zia that PTV—by running such songs—was undermining and mocking the regime's 'Islamic credentials'.[4]

Though PTV and Radio Pakistan immediately stopped playing Nazia and Zoheb songs, their album was easily available in music stores. However, since, in those days, local musicians had to bank a lot on the coverage they got on state-owned media (to generate album sales, and, more so, to tap into the large 'private functions'[5] market), the duo's parents went into overdrive in trying to set up a meeting with the then-Information Minister, Raja Zafarul Haq.[6] After many tries, the Minister then managed to get Nazia and Zoheb an audience with the dictator Zia himself. The teens were summoned to the palatial President House in Islamabad where they were made to sit in front of the grinning General (in full view of PTV's news team and cameras) and were given a long lecture on what it meant to be Muslim and Pakistani. Soon after the meeting, the ban on them was lifted. The duo went on to record and release four more albums.

In a 2012 interview that he gave to a local English daily,[7] Alamgir lamented the compromises that he (and other pop musicians) had to make during the Zia-ul-Haq dictatorship to be able to continue appearing on state-owned television and radio. It was important for these musicians to keep appearing on television because even though they were paid very little money, TV appearances were vital in those days for them to reach out to new audiences and fans who would buy their albums and also attract offers to play at private parties and at other celebratory events. Alamgir said that in 1982 he wasn't allowed to appear on TV in jeans and was asked to 'not move around so much while singing'. Alamgir and Sheikhi were the country's top pop acts but they were entirely dependent on TV since the film industry had collapsed. Ironically, the restrictive Zia era is the period that contains the seeds of what would (a decade later) give birth to 'Pakistan's golden age of pop music'.

By all accounts, the Zia regime was a highly contradictory affair. It is also considered by many to have sown the seeds of a peculiar kind of moral hypocrisy that can still be found across vast sections of Pakistan's polity. On the one hand, the regime's policies were myopic and sometimes outright reactionary, resulting in the banning of various arts (such as Eastern classical, Western and many other forms of dance[8]); and literary works (such as the poetry of Faiz Ahmed Faiz, Ahmed Faraz and Habib Jalib) on TV and radio. On the other, it was during the Zia regime that the use of the VCR and watching Bollywood films at home reached new heights. The contradictory nature of Zia's dictatorship can also be seen in the fact that while some pop idols like Alamgir and Muhammad Ali Sheikhi were being given ample space on TV (albeit, only if they were 'properly attired'), the same regime was banning songs by a teenaged pop/disco duo. Pop music (as long as it was presented within the parameters allowed by the censors) continued to be played alongside the regime's crude political propaganda and the increasing amount of religious programming on PTV.

These parameters included little or no dancing while singing and no physical contact between male and female singers. It was also made known that it was preferable if the singers avoided wearing Western clothes. Also hidden somewhere in such advisories was a distaste for a genre that had started to develop around this time—'Sufi-Pop' (a fusion of Sufi folk music and pop). Pakistan's indigenous and populist 'folk Islam', although popular among the majority of Pakistanis, was scorned at by the puritan minority which was being backed by the Saudi monarchy and Zia.[9] Not only did Zia disapprove of folk Islam on doctrinal bases, his dislike of it also twigged from the fact that the 1970s populism of his late adversary, Z. A. Bhutto, was closely related to the dynamics and politics of the country's folk culture; and that during a 1983 protest movement (the MRD movement—Movement for Restoration of Democracy) against Zia, a number of Sufi shrines in Sindh had become sanctuaries for many young anti-Zia activists.[10]

So it took some convincing by actress-turned-director, Saira Kazmi, when in 1986 she pitched a unique concept to PTV. She wanted to record and direct a video featuring pop star Muhammad Ali Sheikhi, and legendary Sindhi

Sufi folk singer, Allan Faqeer. This was one of the first examples of a modern Pakistan fusion music genre that would become 'Sufi Rock' in the 1990s.[11] Anomalies of this sort kept propping up throughout the repressive dictatorship. Even during what was perhaps the most chaotic and reactionary period of the Zia regime (in 1987)—when the military dictator, after dismissing his own handpicked prime minister, began imposing a second round of harsh and convoluted 'Islamic' legislation—viewers were suddenly treated to a song and video that would trigger the first big wave of urban pop music in the country. The song was the otherwise harmless *Dil Dil Pakistan*, played and sung by a group of middle-class youngsters in Western attire, called Vital Signs.

The director of the video, Shoaib Mansoor, had to struggle to get it played on PTV. In 1988, when Zia died in a plane crash and Benazir Bhutto's Pakistan People's Party (PPP) came to power (through elections), Vital Signs was in the forefront of a number of modern pop acts that took Pakistan by storm. The golden age of Pakistani pop music had finally begun.

While it is true that the sudden popularity of many pop acts at the same time definitely came from the feeling of being liberated from the clutches of state-sanctioned ideas of morality, there was an economic reason behind this phenomenon as well. During the Zia dictatorship, the country had been enveloped in a thick, smoggy façade of strict conservatism and awkward moralistic pretense, even as its urban underbelly was clogged with ethnic tensions, gang violence, corruption and state-sponsored terror initiated by the dictatorship to suppress dissent. Ironically, these political and social tensions and pretensions, power plays and freak economic prosperity—triggered by a 'black economy' which was a mutation of the unprecedented inflow of aid coming in from the US and Saudi Arabia for the 'Afghan Jihad'[12]—propelled the gradual expansion of the country's urban middle and lower-middle-classes.

The youth cultures that emerged from these classes triggered the creation of a kind of pop culture and a music style which we now call 'Pakistani pop'. Between 1988 and 1999, many pop/rock artistes emerged, albums were recorded and released, and more concerts were held than in any other period of the country's history. The trend peaked in the early and mid-1990s, and according to three of Pakistan's largest record labels at the time—EMI-Pakistan, Sonic and Sound Master—some twenty million cassettes and CDs of Pakistani pop bands and solo acts were sold between 1993 and 1995 in the country's four main music markets: Karachi, Lahore, Multan and Rawalpindi.[13] Also, dozens of concerts were held between 1993 and 1996. But from 1998 onwards, things began to change and this phenomenon completely lost steam. Many major bands broke up and many promising acts and groups simply withered away. This happened in part because supply exceeded demand and the pop market reached a state where it began to cannibalise itself.

Also, as the country's economy went into a tail-spin in 1998, multinationals began to pull back their money from the scene and a lot of studios and record labels closed shop. Then, after 9/11, the subsequent violence of militant Islamist groups in Pakistan made it almost impossible for pop concerts to be held, so much so that years after the golden age of pop music in Pakistan folded, we now have a generation that has very little or even no memory of a time when the country actually had a vibrant pop scene and large music concerts were a norm for young Pakistanis. In recent times, as the Pakistani state has attempted to tackle head-on the extremism menace, Pakistani pop is slowly making a comeback, mainly with the help of platforms provided to brand new acts by Coca-Cola, Pepsi and Nescafe.

The new acts of today consider musicians of the golden age like the Vital Signs and guitar genius Aamir Zaki as legends. The Signs, after reigning supreme as the country's leading pop band in the 1990s, broke up in 1998. Much of the band's charm was due to its highly talented and charismatic lead vocalist, Junaid Jamshed. Zaki on the other hand had a cult following. While influential and with a dedicated fan base, Zaki could, however, never quite turn this into the kind of super stardom that men like Junaid Jamshed enjoyed. Junaid quit music in 2002 because he thought Pakistani youth were being exposed to the 'immoralities' that Western music genres came attached with; while the other (Zaki) thought that not enough of these influences were being adopted (and that's why his kind of music had remained a cult phenomenon). Both these highly volatile and talented gentlemen met tragic ends.

I first saw the Signs at a concert at the now defunct Rex Auditorium in Karachi. The year was 1989 and the band had just released their debut album, *VS-1*. The concert hall was packed with young men and women, and, even though many teens were accompanied by their parents, one could still smell whiffs of hashish smoke inside the hall. I befriended Junaid in 1991. I had dropped out of the University of Karachi and joined an English weekly as a political reporter in December 1990. It was the

Signs' second album (*VS-2*) which prompted me to begin dabbling in music journalism as well. Between 1992 and 2001, when I mostly reported and commented on the local pop music scene, I struck up a close affiliation with the Signs, especially with Junaid and the band's keyboardist and leader, Rohail Hayatt. I used to be quite a sight in those days. Shoulder-length hair, unruly beard, wild eyes and fantasies about turning Pakistani pop music into a vessel for some kind of a cultural revolution! In retrospect, it was a naïve notion but at the time it seemed perfectly achievable. Well, at least in my head it was.

Junaid wore his emotions on his sleeves. He loved music. But there was an introverted side to him as well, which the otherwise extroverted Junaid was not quite comfortable with. This conflict between his two sides would continue till he believed he had found a resolution through religion a decade later. Rohail was mostly quiet but very observant and comfortable with his quiet nature. Bassist Shahzad Hassan, too, was of a quiet disposition. By default, Junaid therefore became the band's spokesman. The band's other member, guitarist Rizwan-ul-Haq, who had been brought into the band in 1991, was edgy and circumnavigated with a nervous energy and a largely apprehensive disposition. And his playing, though not spectacular, was incredibly subtle and melodic; perfect for the VS sound which was still developing. But all was not quite well when the band began recording their second album. After recording his vocals, Junaid quit the band, saying he wanted to become an engineer. When Rohail was mixing the new album, the band did not actually exist anymore. This is precisely why the Signs' second album *VS-2* is such a departure from the first album's more upbeat ways. However, 1993 was a happier year for the band as Junaid rejoined. It settled down and began operating as a well-knit unit. It had risen to become Pakistan's top pop act and that too in a then-increasingly competitive pop scene. No wonder on their third album, *Aitebar*, the band decided to rediscover the buoyant mood of the first album.

Rohail was not happy with the band's third album though Junaid was. And in 1994, in the simmering tensions between the two, Rizwan somehow got ousted. Rohail then brought in guitar genius Aamir Zaki. It was an odd choice. While Zaki was technically brilliant and enjoyed a large cult following, his fans couldn't imagine him lasting in the Signs. He didn't. I remember that tensions between the band members were at their peak during the recording of the group's fourth album. In 1994, Rohail quit. Junaid was not amused. Rohail returned in early 1995. But the same year, Zaki was out. He said he couldn't cope with the tensions in the band, and that was saying a lot because Zaki himself was a rather temperamental man. His presence in the Signs always seemed suspect and even atypical.

The recording of the band's fourth album, *Hum Tum*, was therefore a laborious exercise. It took almost a whole year to record. I witnessed much of it as Zaki came and went and then Asad Ahmad, another guitar virtuoso, was brought in to help the band complete the album. Somehow, I felt that this would be the band's last album. I shared this with both Rohail and Junaid. Rohail just shrugged his shoulders. He had worked extremely hard to make this the band's finest album, often working through the night. Junaid was nonchalant about my prediction. He said he had sacrificed too much to see the band wither away after just four albums. He wanted more; he knew he was only now getting better as a vocalist.

And what an album it turned out to be. It was nothing like the serene *Aitebar*. Rohail still calls *Hum Tum* his baby. The production and arrangements on it are dazzling. Like *VS-2*, this album, too, had a lot of ambience and Junaid's vocals are very much part of the atmosphere. The aesthetic and commercial success of the album weren't enough to roll back another happening: Rohail and Shahzad were both emotionally and creatively drifting away from Junaid. Or maybe it was the other way round. They seemed to have nothing in common between them anymore.

The Signs' demise was never officially announced, but in 1998 when the band were offered a deal by Pepsi for another album, Rohail declined, signalling the folding up of what still remains one of the most important and volatile chapters in the history of Pakistani pop music. But, Junaid went on to record three solo albums. I last met Junaid in 2002 during a one-off Signs reunion concert in Karachi. The band had disintegrated in 1998 and Junaid had begun to drift towards more spiritual matters. He had first decided to quit music in 2000, but two years later changed his mind and returned to reform the Signs. Junaid had become a classic example of a young Pakistani who, after he/she feels that they cannot continue to lead a 'Western lifestyle', begins to slide towards adopting a culture (Arab) that too is foreign. Maybe the one between these two is what being a Pakistani means? Maybe.

Just before the comeback concert in 2002, he told me that the band was all set to record a new album. However, right after the concert, he briskly walked into a hall behind the stage and announced that he was quitting music, this time for good. Then walking towards me, he shook my hand and said, 'It's over. Good bye.' We never met again.

Junaid's transformation was not sudden. It was a gradual and rather painful process, unfolding slowly. He was convinced that his future and, more so, the resolution to the inner conflicts he had struggled with lay in becoming a 'born again Muslim'. Incidentally, Junaid's exit from the music scene also marked my exit from music journalism. His departure had nothing to do with mine. It simply symbolised the exit of a generation that had come in riding on an illusion that anticipated the coming of some kind of a post-Zia liberal democratic utopia. But a decade later, this generation had ended up in a vortex of disillusionment. It wanted out. And out it went. Junaid died in a plane crash in 2016.

Zaki, on the other hand, always believed he was too good for the Pakistani audiences. He wanted to play for a more 'informed audience', abroad. I first heard him play in 1987. Fresh out of college in Karachi, I was planning to get into Karachi University (KU) as a student of political science. Much of my previous four years at college had been spent as an activist against the Zia dictatorship. Even though I had been arrested twice and once even tortured, I planned to continue my stint as a student leader at KU. In July 1987, a car bomb had gone off in Karachi's congested Empress Market area, killing dozens of shopkeepers and shoppers. It was a sickening sight; an event directly related to Pakistan's involvement in the Afghan Civil War; an involvement I had been protesting against since my first year in college, in 1984. In August 1987, a college acquaintance, Ozzie, a Pakistani-Christian, George Michael fan, and a pretty decent crooner himself, gave me a cassette of a song recorded by a Pakistani band called The Scratch. Ozzie knew that unlike him, I was more into raunchier music.

'You will like this,' he told me. 'And check out the guitar player.'

There were not many Pakistani bands around in those days. Men such as Alamgir and Muhammad Ali Sheikhi were stars, carefully navigating through the many restrictions imposed on music which was considered to be 'obscene' and 'decadent' by the dictatorship. When I played Ozzie's tape on my Sony Walkman II in August 1987, the Vital Signs had already released their first song *Dil Dil Pakistan*. The song on Ozzie's tape was titled *The Bomb*. It had been written and recorded by Scratch just days after the Empress Market blast. Extremely bluesy and melancholic, what got my immediate attention was the guitar sound. Very Eric Clapton, I thought. Or even Mark Knopfler. Clean, loose and bluesy. I wondered who on earth was playing the guitar like that in Pakistan. The vocals were by a woman, but the lyrics were terrible. A year later, in 1988, a university friend arrived at my house with tickets to a concert at the Intercontinental Hotel (now Pearl Continental). Three bands were to play at this concert near the pool side area of the hotel: Vital Signs, The Scratch and another band. The Signs were yet to release their first album. But I recognised the name, The Scratch and decided to go. We reached the venue which was teeming with teens and twenty-year olds like me. The Signs did not show up. Nor did the other band. But The Scratch did. A guitarist, a bassist, a drummer and a female vocalist in a floral maxi.

They played six songs, all 1980s pop covers. The last one was *Walk Like An Egyptian* by The Bangles. The band did a decent rendition of it, until the guitarist went entirely ballistic during the outro of the song. Switching between long blues leads, raunchy riffs and even some heavy metal stuff, a time came when the rest of his band members just couldn't keep up and simply stopped playing. The guitarist turned around and pressed his guitar over an amplifier to produce a loud feedback sound that must have pierced through and across every room in the hotel. It was nuts. I loved it. I walked up to him after the show. He was quietly packing up his gear: an amp and a yellow and white Fender Stratocaster. The rest of the band were on the other side of the hallway. I told him he was brilliant. He was surprised. I introduced myself and he did, too. His name was Aamir Zaki. And the next evening I was at his place in Karachi's PECHS area.

In his bedroom were posters of Eric Clapton. He was a huge fan, especially of Clapton's *461 Ocean Boulevard* album. Zaki also played the bass, and that too a fretless one preferred by dexterous jazz-fusionists. We talked about the blues, jazz, prog-rock and the works, until we came to *The Bomb*. I told him the lyrics were crap. He agreed and then asked me to write new ones. So I did, right there. He loved them. He picked up an acoustic guitar and set those lyrics to a new version of the song. Right there. Thus began my friendship with this most talented and (as we shall see) also most frustrating musician. I became a journalist in December 1990 and worked as a political and then a crime reporter for a weekly till late 1992. Then, quite accidentally, I became a music critic too. The pop scene in the country had exploded after the demise of Zia in August 1988. Though things did not get any better as far violence and corruption went, the music scene continued to expand, also helped by the fact that certain multinationals began pumping in money into emerging pop acts.

I befriended almost all the new stars. But it was always a musician-critic relationship between us, which blew hot and cold. I always thought they were opportunistic and ungrateful and they believed I was 'unpredictable' and thought of myself as big a star as they were. I did because I was.

My friendship with Zaki, however, was different. We were actually friends. With the music scene expanding, I wanted Zaki to be its leading star. As a teenager, he had already played with the greats, such as Alamgir. By 1993, Zaki had gotten so much better, so flawless, so waiting to just burst out and become the scene's most accomplished player. But he didn't. 'What the hell do you want me to play?' he asked one April evening in 1993. I had told him to stop being this brilliant, misunderstood and reclusive session's player for bygone pop dinosaurs and mediocre jingle-singers. I asked him to assemble a band and jump on the great Pakistani pop bandwagon which had begun to roll into town.

'No musician can keep up with what I want to do, and how I want to play,' he lamented. He wasn't being arrogant. He was right. He was just too goddamn good. Nevertheless, he finally agreed to form a band. He had quit Scratch in 1988. He had spent time honing his talent and playing the odd show with Alamgir. But now a pop musician could actually make some good money through his/her art in Pakistan. So, in 1993, he not only formed a band but also got married. The band was made up of a drummer, a bassist (both Pakistani-Christians), and, of course, Zaki. He asked for a name and I gave him one: Just In Case. It stuck. Zaki was very close to musicians from Karachi's Goan Christian community. These men and women had fallen on hard times after the nightclubs where they had played in the 1960s and 1970s closed down in April 1977. Zaki's love for jazz and classical blues music came from his endearing relationship with Goan Christian musicians. Some of them even played at his wedding at the Intercontinental.

Just in Case failed to take off. As did his marriage. He had married the highly intelligent daughter of a famous playwright and theatre and TV director. It didn't work out. Zaki was too moody, too sulky, and too critical of people he actually cared the most about. He was also very self-critical. I told him he whined too much. He lashed out and responded by telling me that I was hanging out with the 'mediocres' too much. He vanished for the next few months until he called again in November 1994. He told me he had formed another version of Just In Case. It had a guy playing bass, and a real powerhouse drummer. Zaki picked me up from my house and we drove down to the drummer's house. The band jammed non-stop for over three hours. I recorded the session on a tape-recorder. It was intense. The sound was like Rush making out with Cream and then both flirting with Miles Davis. It was awesome, complex and epic. And I told him so. But he complained that the bassist was not able to keep up and the drummer was continuously trying to overshadow the guitar and soon, this edition of Just in Case fell apart as well. Zaki vanished again.

In 1995, after months of silence, I received a call from him.

'NFP, how about coffee?'

'Sure,' I said.

'No, light yourself a cigarette, in fact fix yourself a

drink. You will need it after I tell you what I want to tell you.' He was super excited.

I began to laugh, 'Don't tell me you are getting married again.'

'No, no,' he replied. 'Something even stranger!'

That something 'stranger' was an offer by the Signs to join the band. The Signs, at the time the land's biggest pop act, had ousted their second guitarist, Rizwan-ul-Haq. They now wanted Zaki to be in the group because the Signs' leader, Rohail Hayatt, wanted to expand the band's sound and have a 'more accomplished guitarist'. Zaki asked me whether he should join the Signs. I told him, absolutely. But the truth was, he had already made up his mind. He was going to join and finally taste the pleasures of the mainstream scene. I called Rohail and told him that getting Zaki in the band was a master stroke, even though I had quite liked Rizwan as well. I thought his subtle, melodic style of playing was perfect for the Signs. But Rohail wanted to do something deeper and more complex on the next Signs album. 'A mixture of vintage Eagles and Fleetwood Mac,' he told me. Perfect.

Before and after he joined the Signs, I heard Zaki play on numerous occasions. But I tell you, the way he played with the Signs on the dozen or so concerts that the band played in 1994, was the best I have seen him play. His black Gibson added such a refreshing dimension to all the great Signs songs, making them richer, edgier. Those concerts were such a pleasure to watch. But this was just too good to last. Actually, I knew it could not. At the time, the Signs were going through their own existential crisis, and here was this volatile and moody guitar genius sandwiched between an equally moody (but far more practical) Rohail and a vocalist (Junaid Jamshed) who did not agree with Rohail's idea of 'making a more complex album'. Also, Zaki wanted an equal share of the profits and royalties. Rohail refused.[15] I knew what was transpiring. Rohail requested me not to put it in print because the band was in the process of making an album and was still on Pepsi's payroll.

Zaki drove down to my house and we shared a cigarette on a sidewalk. He seemed calm. Not angry at all. With the Signs, for a bit, he had experienced the rush of the mainstream scene. He had enjoyed it and wanted more of it, but on his own terms. 'Zaki, you should be a star,' I reminded him. Unable to find the kind of musicians who he believed could 'keep up with him', Zaki decided to storm the mainstream all by himself. A few weeks after leaving the Signs, he played me the demo tape he had recorded for his first solo album. On it he played the guitar, bass, keyboards and used a drum-machine. Heck, he even sang.

I loved the songs and the instrumentals. They were driven, and one song, *Mera Pyar* (My Love) was right up there with the most melodic stuff the Signs had done. I asked him who the song was about and he told me, 'someone who doesn't exist and never will'. In mid-1995, he released his first album, *Signature*. I wasn't all that impressed by the final product. He had smoothened it too much. *Mera Pyar* still sounded good, but the rest, though technically perfect, were overproduced. 'This sounds like elevator music played in a dishwasher,' I jokingly told him. 'You should have let the sound leak and bleed through the speakers. And where the heck is the feedback? This is just too clean,' I complained.

He was livid. And, as expected, out came the 'mediocre'

taunt, 'NFP, you have been promoting and listening to the mediocres too much.' I responded by saying that he hadn't used even half of the magic and tricks he possessed as a musician. 'This is repressed stuff, man.' He did not respond. And vanished. However, thanks to the heavy play the video of *Mera Pyar* enjoyed on local pop shows, the album did rather well, bagging him a dedicated cult following. By the late Nineties, the music scene had begun to recede. Falling sales and diminishing multinational interest saw the exit of numerous bands and acts. Many even began to move towards more 'spiritual' callings, joining the Islamic evangelical outfits which had begun to mushroom from the mid-Nineties onwards. I'd had enough as well, suffering from years of substance abuse and those exhausting pretensions of helping to herald in some kind of a cultural revolution through music. My relationship with the eroding music scene collapsed, though I did continue to meet Zaki. He seemed disgusted by the scene. It was not authentic, he rightly pointed out. Then he packed his bags and moved to the US.

A mutual friend, TR, kept me informed about Zaki's stay in the US. He was earning a living by playing in blues and jazz bars. TR told me that there he had finally found the musicians he could relate to (and vice versa). But not for long. In 2000, he was back.

I received a call. It was Zaki.

'*NFP, kya ho raha hai?*' (NFP, what's happening?)

'You are back?' I asked.

'Yes.'

'Now what?' I asked.

'Coffee?'

'Sure.'

We met for coffee. I told him I had cleaned up, gotten married and quit music journalism.

'Those mediocres never deserved the attention you gave them,' he said.

'Perhaps,' I said. 'But you should have been a star.'

He suddenly went quiet and began to stare at a wall behind us. 'I have to go.' Saying this, he just left.

I didn't meet him or hear from him for the next five years.

In 2005, I received a call on my cell phone. I couldn't recognise the number. I answered and it was Zaki.

'NFP, what's up?'

'Zak?'

'Yes. Where have you vanished?'

'Are you the only person allowed to vanish?'

He began to laugh. 'I'm recording again.'

'That's nice, Zak, but I have no clue about the local music scene anymore.'

'I know. I know you quit writing. I quit making music. Too much mediocrity here.'

'Yes,' I replied.

We met that evening and he played me a tape of the songs he had recorded with Hadiqa Kayani. Hadiqa was always a terrific singer. But those songs, they were terrible. Muddy, confused, half-baked. But I remained quiet.

'You didn't like them?' he guessed.

'Zak, this just doesn't work for me.'

He wasn't angry. He just snickered, 'Well, I like them.'

That was the last time I met him. I moved back into journalism (but away from music). There was no music scene to write about anyway. The country was being ripped apart by extremist violence and terrorism. Zaki never made another album. He became a music tutor and would on occasions play small gigs here and there. The concert scene had eroded as well. In 2015, Zaki appeared on the popular TV show, Coke Studio, to play guitar on a song by Zohaib Hassan. I was delighted. But just two days later, I received a call on my cell phone. It was TR. He told me Zaki was in the hospital.

It turned out Zaki had been unwell. I knew he was mentally fragile and extremely moody, but now TR was telling me he needed professional help. Zaki later returned from his latest stint in an institution and it was on that day TR called me again to tell me Zaki wanted to speak to me.

'Hey, NFP,' came a tired voice on my phone.

'Oye, Zak, what have you been doing to yourself?'

'Come over and I'll tell you,' he replied.

'You should have become a star, Zak. You should have let the sound leak and bleed. You should have let it all out. You had so much magic. It is this magic in you which is protesting,' I said.

'Hmm,' came a tired response. 'Come over. We will have coffee. Talk.'

We never did have that talk. I don't know why. Life went on until I saw the headline on dawn.com one morning: 'Aamir Zaki passes away at 49'. The irony of it all is that I was in New Orleans at the time of his passing—the birthplace of jazz and the blues. The two greatest loves of his largely unfulfilled life.

17

Points of Exit

I've been lucky to have been able to travel extensively across Asia, Europe and the United States in the last decade or so. But my favourite destinations are the European cities that I have visited more than once—especially Amsterdam, Berlin and Rome. Long before I managed to visit Europe for the first time, in 2003, I already had a rather romantic perception of the countries in that particular part of the world. I first began to develop this quixotic view about European countries after I joined college in Karachi, in 1983. I had just about started to go around describing myself as a Marxist. But the more I read about the various aspects and variants of communism and socialism, the more I got drawn towards ideas such as 'Euro-Socialism' and the politics of the Welfare State as practised by the Social Democratic parties in Western Europe. But, when finally I did manage to set foot on European soil, in 2003, I had already entered my thirties.

The Cold War was over and European Socialism and the Welfare States that it had spawned were struggling to keep pace with the political and economic shifts that had started to come in after the end of the Cold War (in 1989). More importantly, I was a South Asian man arriving from a bellicose Muslim country at a time when the world had already been turned on its head by the tragic events of 9/11. I wasn't quite sure what sort a reception Europe would give to a man arriving from a country that had begun to be perceived as a 'pariah state', beholden to an ideology that had supposedly made some Arab nuts crash those planes into New York's World Trade Center, in 2001. But in Europe I faced none of what I had feared. Cities such as Amsterdam, Prague, Berlin, Paris, Rome, Naples, London, Istanbul, Barcelona, Lisbon, et al were all very welcoming.

I did all that I could to understand them, not as just another foreign visitor or a tourist, but more as a keen student of cultural and political histories. However, till this day, whenever I am visiting Europe (or even the US), I occasionally do get some awkward glances and questions when after being asked where I am from, I reply, 'Pakistan'. But most of the times the questions in this regard are asked by folk who are genuinely interested in knowing about a mysterious Muslim nuclear power that is not Arab, yet Islamic; militaristic, yet democratic; 'Indianish', but not Indian; and extreme in parts and liberal in others. I do my best to explain the many political, historical and cultural complexities that make Pakistan such an enigma to those who live thousands of miles away from this hotbed of bedlam. Of course, this explanation to them comes from an entirely 'moderate' Pakistani Muslim. I do not roll out knee-jerk apologias for why my country at times hasn't behaved the way a vibrant nuclear-powered democracy should.

I explain things as a Pakistani nationalist, rather,

who tries to clarify that no matter how ragged or 'roguish' Pakistan sometimes seems, it is one of the oldest democracies in the Muslim world whose people are inherently pluralistic, multicultural and enterprising. Nevertheless, every year, during my travels, I find less and less Pakistani rovers on the streets of Europe, the US and even in many Asian countries. The only ones who do travel abroad are those travelling to Dubai or maybe to Malaysia and Turkey, and, of course, Saudi Arabia. But I do come across a healthy number of Indian travellers.

It follows, naturally, that many of the people I meet across Asia, Europe and the US take me for an Indian. This does bother me a little because it brings to light the political and cultural perils of a nation (Pakistan) and a people who have stopped travelling for leisure and for the experience. Wise men across history have rightly emphasised the need for travelling, especially how it opens your mind to things, people and habits outside your own social belief systems; and how this infuses an instinctive realisation in the traveller about the importance of plurality and tolerance; and how tiny, rigid and sometimes rather delusional is the world of an isolationist.

Of course, over the past many years, it hasn't been easy for Pakistanis to obtain visas to a number of countries. Also, the economic situation of the country has made it tough for most Pakistanis to even think about taking a vacation abroad. This is certainly a cause for concern. I say this because the moment you step into another country, you begin to realise that life can indeed be lived without constantly contemplating the fate of a government or the status of one or the other's religious beliefs. By the way, this is something which has suddenly begun to emerge in the US and India as well. I can personally tell my American and Indian friends that this is not such a great space to be in. I know because Pakistan was stuck in such a void for decades. Such voids give birth to a narrow worldview and a standpoint on life which eventually shrinks to the extent that all those venturing into this space are likely to be left with nothing but a constant need to make lofty moral and faith-based judgments and denunciations, believing that they are safeguarding something noble. But this something is nothing more than a convoluted mental construct. This leaves one to believe that his or her culture emerged from a vacuum and that it needs to be 'protected' from 'harmful' external influences. Yet, it is these very outside influences that actually make us whole. I have no qualms in describing myself as a Pakistani nationalist. No qualms at all in calling myself a Muslim. My identity as such is not threatened by these influences. Racial or religious homogeneity or superiority are artificial constructs created to block the many distinct points of entry from where thousands of years of varied cultural, political and religious influences have shaped the meaning of being a Pakistani. Or, for that matter, an Indian or an American.

I've struck some truly fascinating conversations with all kinds of European men and women, and I never hesitate to confess my admiration of how they go about doing things in politics, economics and the arts. I have never faced any episodes of 'Islamophobia' as such. Maybe because I do not go out of my way to exhibit my personal religious beliefs in what I understand and respect to be largely secular societies? Perhaps. But off and on I do experience some rather curious occurrences. For example, once, when I was in the French city of Cannes to represent a Pakistani advertising agency at the Cannes Advertising Festival (in 2009), I was having lunch with my better half at a café just outside the imposing structure in which the festival was being held. Sitting at a table near ours was a middle-aged European couple. A grey-haired man and woman, perhaps French.

The lady kept glancing towards my wife. My wife finally turned sideways and said a soft hello to the lady. This is when the lady turned towards me and asked: 'Where are you both from?' in heavily accented English.

'Pakistan,' I replied, smiling.

'Oh,' the lady's voice rose a bit. 'I've heard that men beat up their wives there!'

Clearly taken aback by the comment, my better half decided to bury her head in the menu card. But I kept looking at the lady who waited for my response. 'Ahem,' I cleared my throat. 'Indeed, we do,' I said. 'In fact I just finished beating up my wife before we came here for lunch. And now I am feeding her so she can get healthy again to face another beating!'

My wife tittered and the lady quickly looked away. Now it was her partner's turn to bury his head in the menu card. Over the course of the lunch, the lady kept stealing glances, until I finally raised my glass of red wine and softly exclaimed, 'Cheers. Here's to wife-beating.'

I shared this episode with a Dutch friend and a German acquaintance, and both were appalled. But we all saw the funny side of it as well. Yes, as a Pakistani, I do come across some awkward moments while travelling in Western countries, but thankfully, such episodes have been extremely rare. On the contrary, on most occasions, as a Pakistani traveller, I have found myself being treated as a somewhat more exotic entity as compared to our more omnipresent South Asian counterparts: Indians.

Whenever I travel now, I look forward to meeting people who are not always judging me through their religious and ideological biases or figuring out where I stand politically. That, however, can be a problem if you are a Pakistani, because then most non-Pakistanis seem to just want to talk to you about your faith as a Muslim. Truth is, I'd much rather talk about music, sports, food, drinks and art. So what do I do? Let them call me an Indian? Sure, I don't have a problem with that, but all they then want to talk about is Bollywood which I don't know much about. So in 2017, when I went travelling again, I decided to introduce myself as a citizen of Surinam!

I got this idea way back in 2005, when, while travelling across Europe, I started talking to an Indian on a plane. He swiftly switched from English to Hindi when I told him that I was from Pakistan. I asked him where he was from in India and he told me that he wasn't from India at all. 'I am from Surinam!' he announced. As it turns out, Surinam, a small country in South America, has a huge 'brown' Hindi-speaking population. So this time that's what I told people in various European countries: 'I'm from Surinam'. And lo and behold, I got what I wanted—lots of discussions on fishing, hurricanes, beaches and drinks. Absolutely nothing on faith, terrorism or wife-beating. A fantastic time I had.

Acknowledgments

I would like to express my gratitude to my parents, Khalida and Farooq (late), and my sister, Roohi. A special thank you to my wife, Amber, for standing by me all these years as I tried to turn writing into a career. It is due to her love, patience and support that I succeeded. Thus, I also want to thank Amber's parents for (finally) saying, yes, when I asked for the hand of their daughter nineteen years ago.

A big thank you to my brother, Adnan, and his wife, Hina as well, for bringing to this world, their beautiful son, Umer—the light of my life who invigorated my interest to write books that can go on to help build a more informed and prouder generation he will one day be a part of.

I would also like to thank mentor and the publisher of my first two books, Najam Sethi; mentors and inspirations, Akbar Zaidi, Imran Aslam and Nichola Khan; my editors at *Dawn*, Zaffar Abbas, Hasan Zaidi and Abbas Nasir; and my former *Dawn* colleagues and supporters, the great late Musadaq Sanwal, and late Murtaza Razvi and friend Raza Rumi. A thank you as well to two of my favourite scholars in Pakistan, Ali Usman Qasmi and Dr Mubarak Ali. A big thank you is also in order for all those friends, colleagues and acquaintances whose lives, words and experiences made this book possible. And also to all those thousands of readers who have remained to be dedicated readers of mine.

Last but not the least, I would like to thank my editor Karthik Venkatesh and Westland Publications for their guidance and interest in taking my book beyond Pakistan.

References

1. A Past in Ruins

1. Maqbool, Aleem, *Could This Ancient City Be Lost?* BBC News, 27 June 2012—http://www.bbc.com/news/magazine-18491900.
2. Possehl, G.L., *The Indus Valley Civilization—A Contemporary Perspective,* Rowman Altamira, 2002, pg. 80.

3. Alcoholic beverages were outlawed in Pakistan in April 1977. However, 'licensed wine shops' were allowed in some parts of Sindh (especially in Karachi) and in the Balochistan province to cater to non-Muslim Pakistanis. Their main clientele, of course, were Muslims!
4. *Sain* in Sindhi is a term of respect akin to 'Mister', but could also be taken to mean 'respectable'.
5. The traditional rugged hybrid slipper-shoe mostly worn by the Pushtuns in Pakistan.
6. *Sindhu* is the ancient name of the river Indus.
7. Muhammad-bin-Qasim (CE 695–715) was an Arab general who conquered the Sindh and Multan regions along the Indus river for a period of time in the eighth century. In recent years, there have been attempts to recast him as one of 'original' founders of Pakistan. This is discussed

in greater detail in Chapter 4 (*My Name Is Pakistan and I'm Not an Arab*).

2. White Heat

1. Arnett, Dr William, *Alexander: A Gayish Biography,* Woodpecker Books, 2015, pg. 30.
2. Cawthrone, Nigel, *Alexander The Great,* Haus Publishing, 2004, pg.108.
3. Zaidi, Ahmad Sajjad, *The Tomb of Shah Rukn-e-Alam* http://www.akdn.org/ky/architecture/project/tomb-of-shah-rukn-i-alam
4. Firasat, S. *The Pathan Population of Pakistan,* European Journal of Human Genetics. 18 October 2006.
5. A distinct dialect of the Punjabi language mostly spoken in southern Punjab and parts of northern Sindh. Some Saraiki scholars treat it as a language separate from Punjabi.

3. A Dry Run

1. A South Asian dish made of kidney beans and boiled eggs.
2. Keown, Damien, *A Dictionary of Buddhism,* Oxford University Press, 2003, pg. 203.
3. Naveed, M.B., *Ancient History Encyclopedia* https://www.ancient.eu/user/mbnaveed15/

4. My Name Is Pakistan and I'm Not an Arab

1. Malik, Basil Nabi, *Jinnah and the religious right, Express Tribune*, 16 January 2011—https://tribune.com.pk/story/104683/jinnah-and-the-religious-right/
2. Asif, Manan Ahmed, *A Book of Conquest: The* Chachnama *and Muslim Origins in South Asia,* Harvard University, 2016 pg. 163.
3. Asif, Manan Ahmed, *The Advent of Islam in Pakistan* in

A *History Of Pakistan* (Editor: Roger D. Long). Oxford University Press, 2015.

4. Ibid.
5. Asif, Manan Ahmed Asif, *A Book of Conquest: The* Chachnama *and Muslim Origins in South Asia,* Harvard University, 2016. pg. 162.

5. Dubious Ancestors

1. Historians who re-interpret historical records thus challenging orthodox views.
2. Dani, Ahmad Hasan, *Pakistan Through the Ages,* Sang-e-Meel Publications, 2007.
3. *Ancestry DNA of a Pakistani*—youtube video—https://www.youtube.com/watch?v=_IXwp3TKjR8&app=desktop
4. Ali, Dr Mubarak, *Pakistan in Search of Identity*, Aakar Books, 2011.
5. Term coined in 1980 by American scholar Martin Kramer to describe activities of individuals and organisations wanting to transform the state and society according to so-called Islamic rules and laws.
6. Cann, Rebecca Louise, Stoneking Mark, and Wilson, Allan Charles Wilson *Mitochondrial DNA and Human Evolution,* 1987—https://embryo.asu.edu/pages/mitochondrial-dna-and-human-evolution-1987-rebecca-louise-cann-mark-stoneking-and-allan

6. A Saint's Journey

1. G.M. Syed had advocated the separation of Sindh from Pakistan in 1972.
2. Burton, Sir Richard, *Sindh and the Races that Inhabit the Valley of the Indus*, 1851.
3. Boivin, Michel and Cook, Matthew (Editors) *Interpreting the Sindh World*, Oxford University Press, 2010.

7. A Matter of Land

1. Sinha, B., *South Asian Transnationalism*, Routledge, 2014, pg. 122.
2. Tiwari, S., *Contemporary Indian Dramatists*, Atlantic Publishers, 2007, pg. 75.
3. Chaurasia, R.S., *History of Medieval India* Atlantic Publishers, 2002, pg. 52.
4. Anand, A., *History Discussion*, Articles Resource website, 2016.

8. The Minister of the Kitchen

1. *Dawn,* 27 August 2014, and *Express Tribune*, 4 June 2012.
2. Ibid.
3. Historical statistics published in The Karachi City Government website on 13 February 2008 (http://www.pbs.gov.pk)
4. *The History of Mughal Cuisine through Cook Books*, The Heritage Lab, 23 January 2017.
5. Black, Cyril E., Dupree, Louis and Elizabeth M., *The Modernization of Inner Asia*, Taylor & Francis, 2016.
6. Genghis and Chagatai were followers of Tengrism, also known as Tengriism or Tengrianism, a Central Asian religion characterised by shamanism, animism, totemism, poly- and monotheism and ancestor worship.
7. The largest Muslim sect.
8. According to the *Concise Encyclopedia of Languages & Linguistics of the World* (Elsevier Publications, 2014) 'Hindustani' began to develop in the thirteenth century and was initially known as 'Hindavi'.
9. Garcia M., *Urdu Evolution and Reform*, Punjab University, 2015, pg. 223.
10. Ali, Dr Mubarak, *Pakistan in Search of Identity* Aakar Books, 2011, pg. 14.

11. Ibid.
12. Ibid pgs. 15-16.
13. Mohajir in Urdu means 'refugee'. This was the term used for the millions of Urdu-speaking Muslims who migrated from India to the newly created Pakistan in 1947. The term became a moniker for those whose first language was Urdu and mostly settled in Sindh's urban centres (especially Karachi and Hyderabad).
14. Fazal Abul, *Ain-e-Akbari* (First written in 1590)
15. Launched as the Mohajir Qaumi Movement in 1984.

9. A Return to the Womb

1. An aggressive rock music genre which emerged from Seattle in the United States and became all the rage in the early 1990s.
2. Muhammad, Shan, *Sir Syed Ahmad Khan: A Political Biography*, University of California, 1969, pg. 20.
3. *The Constitution of the Khilafah State,* Hizbut Tarir, 2011 (a propaganda booklet of the HuT).
4. *The New Statesman* (5 November 2008).

10. Their Man from Africa

1. Gayer, L., *Ordered Disorder and the Struggle for City*, HarperCollins, 2016, pg. 268.
2. A ruler of the then-independent state of Kalat in present-day Pakistan province of Balochistan.
3. Askari, S., *Studies on Karachi* Cambridge Scholars Publishing, 2016.
4. Kwekudee, K., *Blacks in Pakistan,* Down Memory Lane, 23 August 2012.
5. Jayasuria, S. and Pankhurst, R., *The African Diaspora in the Indian Ocean,* Africa World Press, 2003.
6. Pandya, Y. and Rawal, T., *The Ahmedabad Chronicle—Imprints of a Millennium,* Vastu Shilpa Foundation.

7. Kwekudee, K., *Blacks in Pakistan,* Down Memory Lane, 23 August 2012.
8. Pinto, J., *Slavery in Portuguese India,* Himalaya Publishing House, 1992, pg. 97.
9. Shah, A.M., *African Descendants with Indian Admixture*, American Journal of Genetics, July 2011, pg. 154.
10. *Sindh and the Races that Inhabit the Valley of The Indus* (First published in London in 1851).
11. Kwekudee, K., *Blacks in Pakistan,* Down Memory Lane, 23 August 2012.
12. Hughes, A.W., *The Sindh Gazetteer,* George Bell & Sons, 1874.
13. *The News International*, 7 July 2008.
14. Crump, M. and Fenolio D.B., *Eye of Newt & Toe of Frog*, University of Chicago Press, 2015 pg. 255.
15. *The Friday Times*, 4 May 2012.
16. 'Tickets in black' is a phenomenon peculiar to the subcontinent. When single-screen theatres were the norm in Pakistan and India, local toughs would buy tickets in bulk for popular movies and then sell them at a premium or 'in black' which was the colloquial term. This practice has disappeared with the arrival of multiplexes.
17. *The Friday Times*, 4 May 2012.
18. *Herald*, 30 April 2012.
19. *The News*, 30 April 2015.
20. Potter, L.G., *Sectarian Politics in the Persian Gulf,* Oxford University Press, 2014, pg. 236.

11. A Band's End

1. *Census of India Report* 2011.
2. *International Business Times*, 7 August 2013.
3. Henn. A. *Hindi-Catholic Encounters in Goa*, Indiana University Press, 2014.

4. Hamilton, Edward, *Gazetteer of Sindh Province*, Mercantile Press, 1919 pgs. 3-4.
5. Tariq S., *The Role of Christians in the Freedom Movement of Pakistan*, Pakistan Journal of Social Sciences, 2012, pg. 437.
6. Khan, Nicolha (editor), *Cityscapes of Violence in Karachi*, Oxford University Press, Pakistan, 2016.
7. Paracha, Nadeem Farooq, *End of the Past,* Vanguard Books, 2016, pg. 122.
8. *Dawn*, 4 December 2015.

12. Escaping Mao

1. *Dawn*, 9 July 2001.
2. *The News International,* 6 December 2007.
3. Ibid.
4. *Asian Times*, 17 May 2017.
5. *Express Tribune*, 22 May 2015.
6. Ibid.
7. Situated in Karachi, this graveyard was built by British colonialists to bury British officers and officials serving in Karachi. It then increasingly begun being used as the burial ground for deceased Pakistani-Christians.

13. The Indus Raga

1. The Indus Valley Civilisation (See Chapter 1).
2. Classical Sufi/esoteric Muslim poetry.
3. Shackle, C., *Sufi Lyrics,* Harvard University Press, 2015.
4. Ahmad, S., *Great Sufi Wisdom*, Adnan Books, 2004, pg. 175.
5. Arbab, M., *Sufi Saints of Indus Valley*, Lulu Publishers, 1992, pg. 92.
6. Ibid.
7. Hari, Dr R.M., *Some Moments With The Master*, Bookbay, 2012.

8. *The Inner Voice,* 15 June 2008.
9. *Dawn*, 17 April 2014.
10. Hazrat Ali, a close companion of Islam's Prophet.
11. I was told this by Sufi singer, poet, journalist and my good friend, late Musadiq Sanwal, in 2011.

14. Drinking Lessons

1. Udupa, S. and McDowell, S.D., *Media As Politics in South Asia*, Taylor & Francis, 2017, pg. 41.
2. *India Today*, 15 March 1978.
3. My father, who was present at that Press Conference narrated this incident to me.
4. *Dawn*, 10 February 1979.
5. *The Washington Post*, 1 June 2004.
6. *Daily Telegraph*, 24 May 2014.
7. Ibid.
8. Hassan, J., *Islam: Law & Society*, Federation Press, 2011, pg. 44.
9. Khawaja, J., *Authenticity & Islamic Liberalism,* Allied Publishers, 1987, pg. 22.
10. *Dawn*, 2 March 2017.
11. *The News*, 20 March 2017.
12. Haider, W. and Chaudhry, W.M., *Prevalence of Alcoholism in the Punjab*, Biomedica, 2008, pgs. 80-84.
13. Ibid.
14. Ibid.
15. Bose, D.K., *Wine in Ancient India* Conner Calcutta, 1922.
16. Ibid.
17. Psychology Today (15 June 2011).
18. Conrad, Chris, *Hemp For Health*, Healing Hearts Press, 1997.
19. Booth, M. *Opium: A History*, Simon & Schuster, 1996.
20. Restivo, S. (editor), *Science, Technology & Society*, Oxford University Press, 2005.

21. Bose, D.K., *Wine in Ancient India,* Conner Calcutta, 1922
22. Ibid.
23. Craig, A.M., *Heritage of World Civilization*, Pearson Prentice Hall, 1999, pg. 100.
24. Eraly, A., *The Age of Wrath*, Penguin Books, 2015.
25. Ibid.
26. Ibid.
27. Ansari, M.A., *Social Life of the Mughal Emperors*, University of Michigan, 1974, pg. 33.
28. Eraly, A., *The Mughal World*, Penguin Books, 2007.
29. Ibid.
30. Ibid.
31. Asopa, V.N., *India's Global Tea Trade*, Allied Publishers, 2011, pg. 6.
32. Eraly, A., *The Mughal World*, Penguin Books, 2007.
33. Foster, Sir William (editor), *The Embassy of Sir Thomas Roe in India*, Oxford University Press, 1926.
34. Chopra, H. and Nanda, C., *Text Book of Cardiology*, Jaypee Brothers, 2013, p. 298.
35. Venkatachalapaty, A.R., *In Those Days There Was No Coffee*, Yoda Press, 2006, pg. 33.
36. Eraly, A., *The Mughal World*, Penguin Books, 2007.
37. Ibid.
38. *Calcutta Review*, January 1898.
39. *Biomedica,* Vol. 24 July 2008.

15. Wearing the Inside Out

1. West, B., *Encyclopedia of the Peoples of Pakistan*, Infobase Publishing, 2009, pg. 629.
2. Stein, B., *A History of India*, Blackwell Publishing, 1998, pg. 47.
3. Bauazizi, A. and Weiner, M., *State, Religion & Politics of Afghanistan, Pakistan and Iran*, Syracuse University Press, 1986, pg. 355.

4. Moghadam, V., *Gender and National Identity*, Palgrave, 1994, pg. 76.
5. Ibid.
6. *Dawn*, 9 December 2010.
7. Dani, Ahmad Hasan, *Pakistan Through the Ages,* Sang-e-Meel Publications, 2007.

16. It Came from the West

1. See Chapter 11.
2. *Express Tribune*, 22 April 2015.
3. It was called this by a pop music critic, M. Ali Tim, in 1991, and caught on.
4. *The Herald,* Volume 36, 2005.
5. Private parties, corporate dinners, weddings.
6. *The Herald,* Volume 36, 2005.
7. *The News*, 14 March 1996.
8. Hemani, S., *Representing Pakistan Through Folk Music & Dance*, University of Alberta, 2011, pg. 120.
9. Commins, D., *The Wahabi Mission & Saudi Arabia*, IB Tauris, 2009.
10. Mushtaq, A.Q., *Movement For The Restoration of Democracy*, GCC University.
11. The term was first coined by me in 1993 and it gradually took hold.
12. *Asia Survey*, Volume 31, 1991.
13. *The News*, Political Economy section, 5 April 1997.
14. *Dawn*, 18 December 2016.